Garden Shrubs and Trees

Janet Browne
and Brian Ward

Macdonald Guidelines

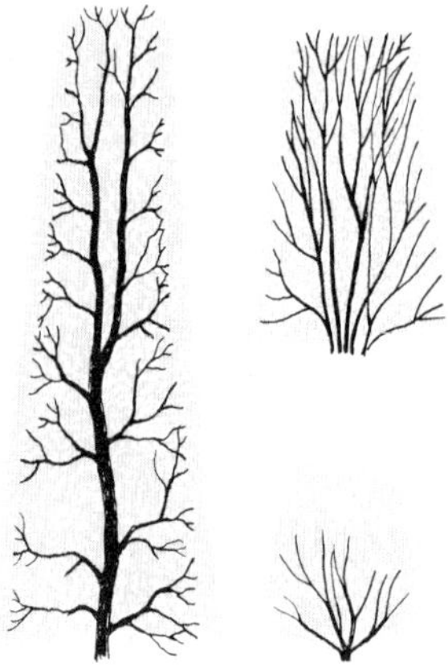

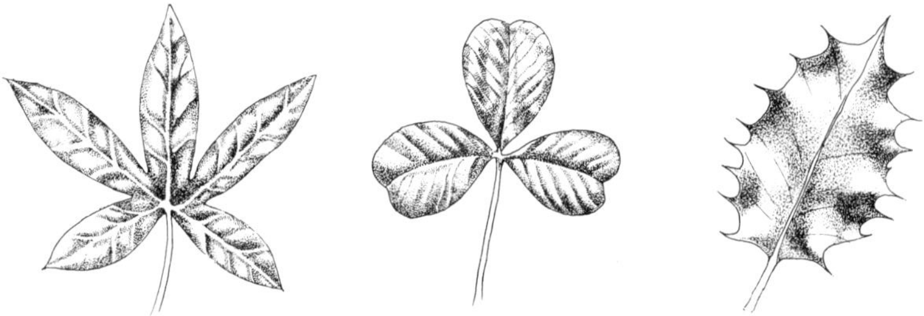

Editorial manager
Chester Fisher
Series editor
Jim Miles
Editor
Alan Wakeford
Designer
Robert Wheeler
Picture researcher
Jan Croot
Production
Penny Kitchenham

Contents

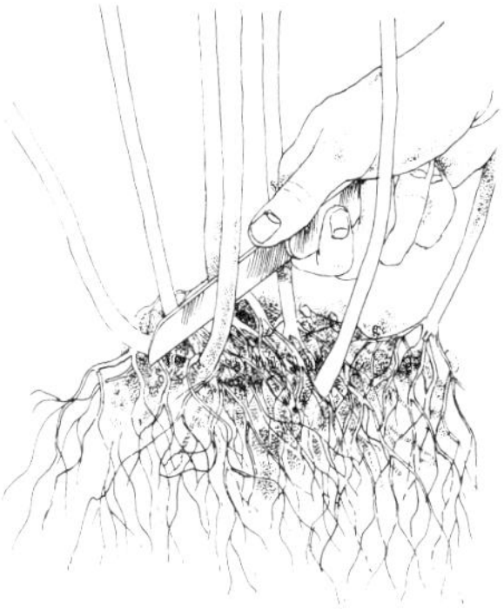

First published 1979
Macdonald Educational Ltd
Holywell House
Worship Street EC2A 2EN

ISBN 0 356 06035 7
(paperback edition)
ISBN 0 356 06435 2
(cased edition)
Printed and bound by
Waterlow (Dunstable)
Limited

The plant collectors

Shrubs and trees have been grown for thousands of years and today, as a result of dedicated plant hunters scouring the world for new species, there are hundreds of plants suitable for decorating both small and large gardens. But where did these plants come from and how did they get to us? Unfortunately, the earliest civilizations kept few details about shrubs and trees they cultivated and the areas to which they were introduced. It was not until 5,000 years ago in the Middle East that early plant hunters began to collect and record plants from areas well away from their homeland.

The early plant hunters

Egyptian pharoahs and queens were probably the first plant hunters. The pharoah Sankhara, for example, sent trading expeditions down the Red Sea to the Gulf of Aden, and to other parts of the Middle East. These returned with beautiful and useful plants which eventually became naturalized in the Nile Valley. In 1482 BC, Queen Hatshepsut sent five ships to the Land of Put (somewhere off the East African coast) to obtain frankincense (boswellia), and on their return 31 trees were successfully established in the Temple Gardens at Thebes. Her slaves also brought back many other seeds and plants using reed baskets and jars to transport them in soil. A few years later, Thutmosis III, the queen's successor, returned from Syria with even more plants and, although most cannot be identified, 275 are illustrated on the walls of his Botanic Room in the temple at Karnak.

Between then and the 4th century BC, merchants trading spices probably carried plants to and from various countries. And during Roman times plants were moved fairly freely in the European world. In particular there was a good trade for rose bushes from Greece, Persia and Afghanistan, and plants such as the plane tree, lime, damson and mulberry were all well known.

The Middle Ages

Up to the 11th and 12th centuries AD, it appears that there was little movement in plants, except for those used medicinally. However, as a result of the Crusades, oranges, pomegranates, cedars, cypress, olives and myrtle were seen in Europe for the first time. It was shortly after this that Albertus Magnus (1193–1280), perhaps the first scientific plant hunter, worked, systematically observing and recording plants of large areas of Europe.

The Renaissance period

This awakening of interest in plants accelerated during the 15th and 16th centuries as species were grown other than those in monastery herbal gardens. The plant hunters of this period include the Germans Von Cube, Brunfels and Fuchs, the Swiss Gesner, the English William Turner, the Italian Pier Mattioli, the Flemming de Busbecq and

▶ A well planned selection of trees, shrubs and climbers does much to enhance the appearance of any garden by giving a variety of shapes and forms as well as colour throughout the year.

▲ Gardens were important to the Moghuls, as seen in this miniature painting, c.1600, of young Shah Jahan entertaining learned men in a tree designed area.

the Dutch Clusius, Dodonaeus and Lobelius. Botanical centres were also started, Padua being the first followed by others in Basle, Strasbourg, Bonn, Cologne and Bologna, and there was an increase in the traffic of plants among the various European countries.

'The Golden Age of Botany'

After a lull in the 17th century, the 18th century again saw plant hunting in full spate and it has often been referred to as 'The Golden Age of Botany' for systematic searches of plants, classification and botanical experiments. With improvements in travel between the continents and the patronage of royal or rich men, botanists were able to go further afield to seek and study plants. Many species were then sent to botanical or private gardens, or to plant nurseries. There was also a considerable interchange of plants by sea between collectors and thus it was that gardens all over the world began to be enriched by plants from foreign lands.

Many of the plants, however, never survived their long overland or sea journey as no method had been devised to overcome the enormous variations in climate and travelling conditions. Seeds stood a better chance of surviving so plant houses or orangeries, as they were often called, were built in which to raise the plants and give them growing conditions as closely related as possible to their natural environment.

There are so many plant hunters from the 18th century onwards that it is difficult to mention them all. One, who played a large part in the exchange of plants between North America and England is John Bartram, now remembered for his botanical gardens in the Philadelphia Park near the Schuykill River. Philbert de Commerson of France also travelled extensively and thought nothing of stealing plants if he couldn't obtain them by fair means. He is thought to have been the first to introduce the hortensia hydrangeas, and he also claimed knowledge of thousands of plants from Australia, South America, Mauritius and Madagascar. At the same time Linnaeus (Carl von Linne) from Sweden was active in Northern Europe. The 'Father of Modern Botany', it was he who realized the limitations of existing plant nomenclature and introduced the binomial system (see page 15) which is still in use today. Towards the end of the century, although strictly forbidden by the Chinese and Japanese, various people, such as the Englishman Cunningham, the Swede Thunberg and missionaries and staff of trading posts, managed to smuggle out of China and Japan plants including *Berberis thunbergii*, camellias, paeonies and azaleas.

The 19th and 20th centuries

The Scottish collector, David Douglas, who explored mainly in the Americas is best remembered for his introduction into Europe of the Douglas Fir, *Abies grandis*, in 1830. Other plants he is known for include acers, arbutus and pinus. Douglas was probably the last well-known plant hunter to suffer from the problem of getting his species home. Transport by sea or overland was still hazardous and it is amazing that so many plants still survived. However, with the development of terraria or Wardian cases (named after Dr Nathaniel Ward, who discovered that plants grown in glass-stoppered jars appeared to live healthily for an indefinite period) shrubs and trees were able to survive long journeys.

From this time onwards the movement of plants round the world was immense. Even China and Japan opened their countries to plant-hunting expeditions, and it was from the Far East generally that new species were introduced. Von Siebold, from Germany, for example, introduced hamamelis, ilex and wisteria among others, while the Scot Robert Fortune brought to England some 120 new species or varieties of plants including lonicera, forsythia, rhododendron and skimmia. Three other famous plant hunters not to be forgotten are Ernest Wilson, who spent most of his life in America, George Forrest, who introduced more than 300 new species of rhododendrons and Frank Kingdon-Ward, who introduced about 100 more rhododendrons.

▲ Linnaeus (1707–78) was known as 'The Father of Modern Biology' at Uppsala University, Sweden, following the publication of his *Species Plantarum* which introduced the binomial system of plant nomenclature.

Other now popular plants discovered by these three include buddleia, clematis, cornus and hypericum.

Today people are still finding new genera and species of plants all over the world, albeit not in such great quantities as previously. But given the great interest there is in growing shrubs and trees, the main emphasis is on plant breeding and the development of new varieties and hybrids possibly more suited to local conditions.

The biology of shrubs and trees

Trees and shrubs for the garden range from those suitable as single specimens, reaching a height of seven metres or more, down to the tiny prostrate or alpine types which superficially do not even resemble what they are supposed to be. The technical definition of a tree is that it has a woody stem or stems. A tree has a single stem at ground level which may branch very quickly whereas a shrub has numerous woody stems. In practise, however, the distinction is not important. Some very large shrubs develop into tree-like proportions, and conversely, many trees branch so close to the ground that their trunk is all but invisible.

Like all other flowering plants, shrubs and trees are based on the same pattern of leaves, stems and roots, and understanding the biology of these plants makes obvious some of the measures needed to keep them healthy. Except for the parasitic mistletoe, all trees and shrubs are rooted into the ground. The diameter of the root spread is

◀ Root hairs penetrate between soil particles (**1**), absorbing nutrients from the thin film of water covering them. From the roots, liquid passes up the stem or trunk through tubular vessels (**2**). Water evaporates from the tiny pits called stomata on the underside of the leaves (**3**) and the nutrients it carries, under the influence of sunlight, produce sugars on which the plant feeds.

about the same as the height of the plant and the depth the roots reach depends upon the type of shrub or tree and the structure of the soil. In a really large tree such as the oak, needing a large amount of mechanical support, more than half the bulk of the whole tree lies in the roots. The root system serves to absorb water and minerals from the soil, passing them up through the hollow vessels in the stems or trunk to the leaves where they will be used to manufacture the food used by the plant. In all shrubs and trees the outer layer of the stems becomes covered with protective bark, and vessels deeper within the stem become filled with hard material which supports the stems.

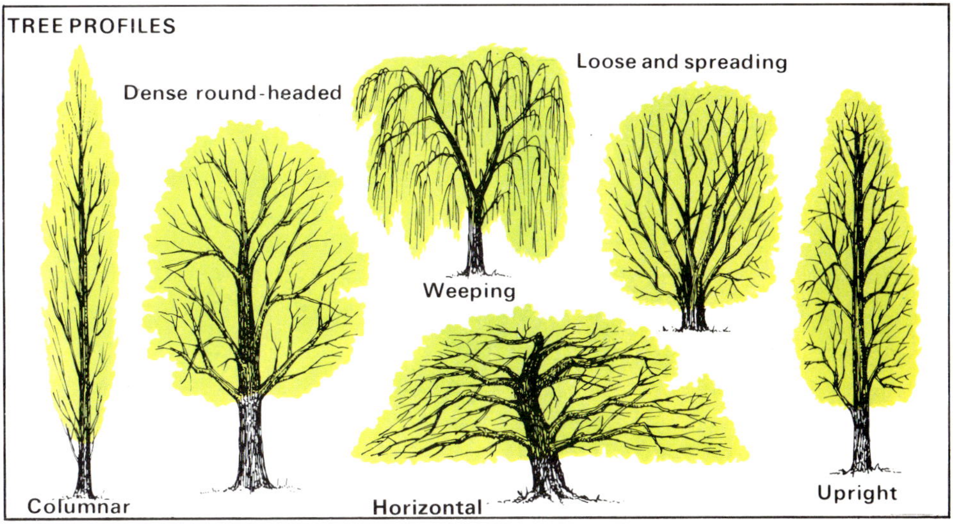

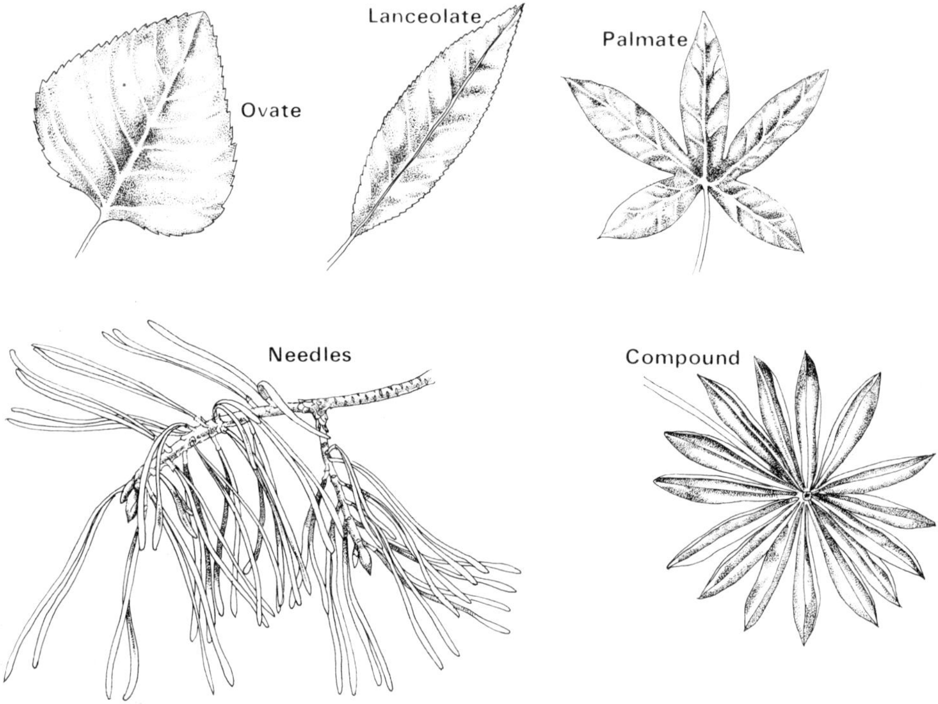

Leaf shapes

In the leaves of a shrub or tree, the process of photosynthesis provides life-giving nutrients for the plant. Leaves are chemical factories, supplied with raw materials in the liquid drawn up from the roots, and by oxygen and carbon dioxide gas present in the air. Sunlight provides the fuel needed to convert these materials into the sugars needed to support plant life. The whole leaf is modified to help this process and the way in which it is modified is what gives it its characteristic shape, colour and consistency.

Leaves are always fanned out to catch the largest possible amount of sun. In fact, they actually swing round to follow its movement during the day. To increase the leaf area exposed to the sun still more, the leaf is often split up or divided into smaller leaflets spread about a central stem, or it may be serrated. The shape and description is an important characteristic of each type of shrub and tree. A typical leaf has a central stem or petiole supporting the flat blade. This petiole splits into smaller veins containing conducting vessels. Such a leaf is referred to as being palmate, oval or lanced-shaped, while leaves with separate leaflets arranged along the petiole are called pinnate.

Within the blade of the leaf are tiny packets of the chemical chlorophyll, called chloroplasts. Chlorophyll, which is green in colour, is the material which uses the light falling on the leaf to transform the simpler chemicals present into useful nutrients. It is based on iron, and if this is deficient in the soil, the plant will be unable to make enough chlorophyll and will be pale coloured or chlorotic. This condition also arises when iron is present in a form which the plant cannot use.

Over the upper surface of the leaf is a waxy layer or cuticle, which stops the water in the leaf evaporating too fast. This cuticle gives leaves such as holly and laurel their characteristic glossy surface. However, it is necessary for some water to evaporate in a controlled way in order for movement of water through the stem and roots to take place. This happens through the shaded lower surface of the leaf, where sunlight is less intense. Tiny apertures called stomata regulate the evaporation and absorption of water, and the entry and escape of gases used or produced by the plant.

Trees and shrubs are classed as deciduous or evergreen, depending on whether they retain their leaves throughout the winter. Deciduous plants often show beautiful colour changes in autumn, as nutrients are withdrawn from the leaves before they drop. In many evergreen plants, such as conifers, the leaves are reduced to fine needles with no clearly defined upper or lower surface. This has the effect of increasing their area still further. Some leaves have shapes with sharp spines developed along the edges, while in variegated types areas of the leaf are lacking in chlorophyll, although if they are grown in poor light, the plant compensates by turning these white or yellow areas green.

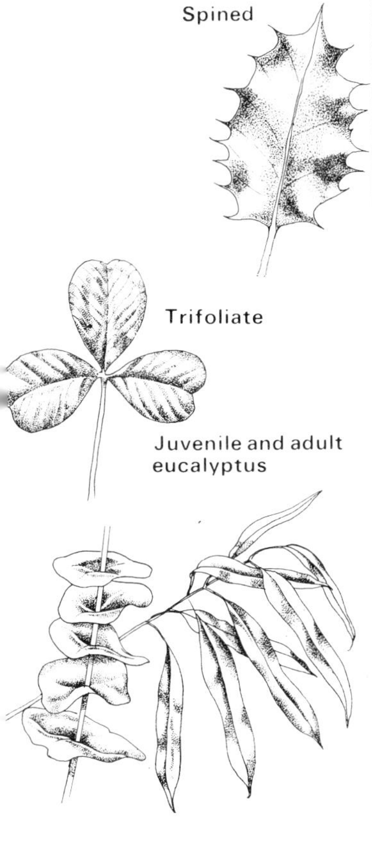

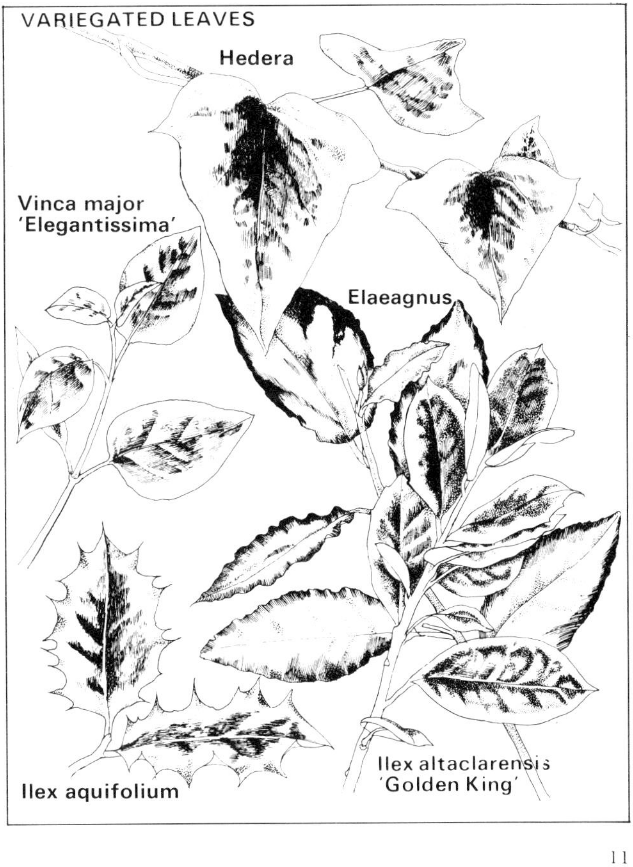

Flowers

Although many are grown purely for their foliage, all the shrubs and trees kept in gardens are flowering plants. This includes conifers, as the cones act as very crude flowers. The flower is the most important reproductive organ of the plant. Although most plants can also reproduce vegetatively (i.e. by shoots, runners or any other part of the plant which can become rooted and subsequently be separated into a new plant), flowers are the means by which the plant reproduces sexually. Fertilization is carried out by pollen which must reach the plant's ovum to start developing into a seed, and the flower is the specially modified mechanism in which this process occurs.

Primitive flowers rely on huge amounts of wind-blown pollen reaching the ovum and completing fertilization, as in all conifers, simple flowers such as the birch and hazel catkin, and the flowers of most of our native trees. Shrubs and trees with decorative flowers rely on insects carrying the pollen and the flowers are designed to help this process by producing attractive scents, nectar or colours and patterns which attract bees and other pollinating insects.

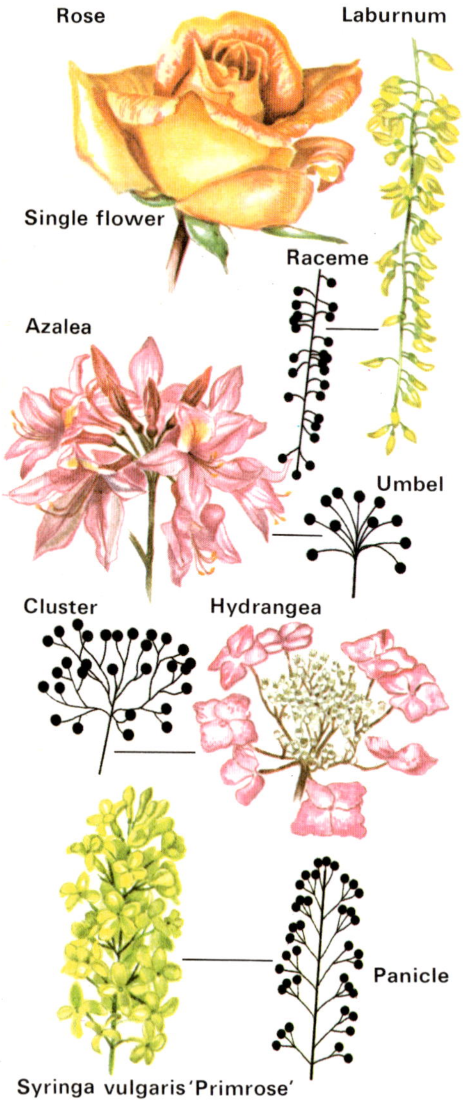

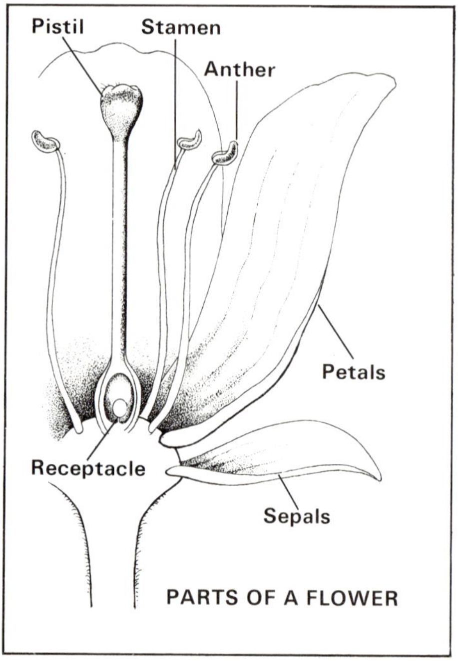

PARTS OF A FLOWER

▲ Many of the most decorative plants flower heavily in spring. Select them carefully to ensure a good range of colours.

◀ Trees and shrubs can still be highly decorative in autumn and winter.

Flowers may be either male, producing pollen; female, with the ovum; or, more frequently, have both elements present in the same flower. Their structure is always basically the same, with the components arranged in rings, with sepals on the outside, petals within them, stamens or male organs next, and the female receptacle (the ovum) in the centre. The petals are not always the decorative part. Sometimes the sepals may be coloured and in some varieties the stamens have been modified into petals. Other flowers have brightly coloured leaves or bracts resembling petals.

Seeds, berries, fruits and other features

The fertilized ovum of a shrub or tree is capable of growing into a new plant. However, this seed is usually enclosed in another structure derived from the receptacle of the flower. The whole fruit consists of seeds or seed, plus the receptacle, which is usually developed in some specialized way.

The fruit is often in the form of a berry, brightly coloured to encourage the birds to eat it and so spread the seeds to new growing areas. It can also be modified in any number of special forms intended to help the distribution of the seed, and some of these are highly decorative. The majority of berries are red or orange, such as those of cotoneaster, pyracantha and holly. However, others, such as pernettya, callicarpa and symphoricarpos, have unexpected bright colours which can make them look like wax. Because berries are produced late in the season, such plants are especially valuable to provide a splash of colour at a time when most plants have finished flowering.

A few plants with larger decorative fruits are also grown. These include the crab apple, malus and the so-called japonica, chaenomeles, but for many such plants it is the flowers which are the real attraction, and the fruits come as an added bonus. Many species of rose are available apart from the common cultivated varieties.

▼ Species of rosa can be selected for their highly decorative autumn fruits.

Names of plants
In order to simplify the confusion over plant names, the Swedish botanist, Linnaeus, in 1753, introduced a standard method of classification. His binomial nomenclature is still in use today and since the 18th century botanical congresses have been held regularly to revise the rules for naming plants. Each plant has now a Latin 'surname' (the generic name) and a 'christian' name (the specific name) and these will identify the plant anywhere in the world. The full name of a plant is generally given in the following order:
Genus will encompass a selection of closely related plants, e.g. rosa, where there are many similar species and varieties.
Family: e.g. rosaceae, includes every genus that is closely related, such as cotoneaster, crataegus, prunus, pyrus and many others.
Common name: e.g. rose for rosa.
Species (specific names): written in italics e.g. *Rosa foetida*.
Variety name: follows the specific name and is italicized if the plant occurred naturally in the world, e.g. *Rosa foetida bicolor*.
Cultivar or variety name: where the plant has been developed in cultivation the name is put in single quotes after the specific names, e.g. *Rosa gallica* 'Officinalis'.
Hybrids: crossings of species or hybrids are listed with an 'x' between the generic name and the hybrid, e.g. *Rosa* x *centifolia* or with the generic name in single quotes, e.g. Rosa 'Peace'.
Form: loosely refers to varieties or types of plants.
Synonym (syn.): indicates the name by which a genus, family or individual plant used to be known.

▲ The waxy berries of skimmia are bright red against darker evergreen leaves.

Some produce enormous decorative hips which persist well into winter, providing an array of colour.

Still more shrubs and trees are grown for the colour produced by other parts of the plant. The smoke bush, cotinus, is attractive in its own right, but its best feature is the mass of feathery flowering plumes which persist on the shrub long after the true flowers have died off, looking like a shimmering cloud of smoke. In other shrubs, the stems themselves are attractively coloured, as in the dogwood, cornus, where the new growth is coloured bright red or purple.

Garden planning and preparation

Gardening with shrubs and trees is going to mean a certain investment in time and effort—possibly more than the initial amount of work needed to set up a garden specializing in the usual types of annual flowers and bedding plants. But once the shrubs and trees are established as part of a garden containing all types of plants, the upkeep and maintenance needed is minimal. They will not need constant replanting and require little routine attention other than pruning.

Your garden may be currently quite tidy, needing only some readjustment before planting decorative shrubs and trees. Possibly it is a new garden, however, littered with lumps of brick, clay and dried cement, and only roughly levelled. There is no substitute for hard work here. Remove all obstructions and rubbish, including doubtful trees or shrubs. You can probably arrange for your local council to remove the rubble. Burning of old trees and weeds is not a good idea, although ash can sometimes be beneficial to the soil

If you have an established but heavily overgrown garden, your problems are similar. Be quite ruthless; demolish old sheds which are past repair, and cut back all the soft growth and weeds until you can examine any interesting shrubs or trees properly. Some may be worth saving. Identify them carefully and, if you want to keep them, prune and reshape as shown on pages 34 to 39. Many straggly shrubs will benefit from severe cutting back. Trees which have outgrown their position can sometimes be pollarded. This entails cutting off the whole of the top to reduce the height and make them bush out. If this is not possible, and the tree is obviously too large or obtrusive, it may have to go—but check with your local council first to make sure that it is not listed and protected.

Planning

Now your garden is roughly cleared, decide on the type of garden you are going to create. Make a list of the features you are hoping to include; raised beds, paths, patio, rock garden and pond, etc. Next you must measure the overall size of the garden and mark this outline on a large sheet of graph paper, using a convenient scale such as 1cm:2m. Mark the position and size of the house and fixed features, such as large trees, drain covers and any eyesores which may need to be concealed or screened. Now you can begin to sketch in the positions for the trees, shrubs and other features you are planning, remembering that the large plants will quickly spread. This means

▼ Drawing up a garden plan on graph paper is worth the small amount of effort involved. As you pencil in the plants you will be adding, it is easy to make allowance for their future spread.

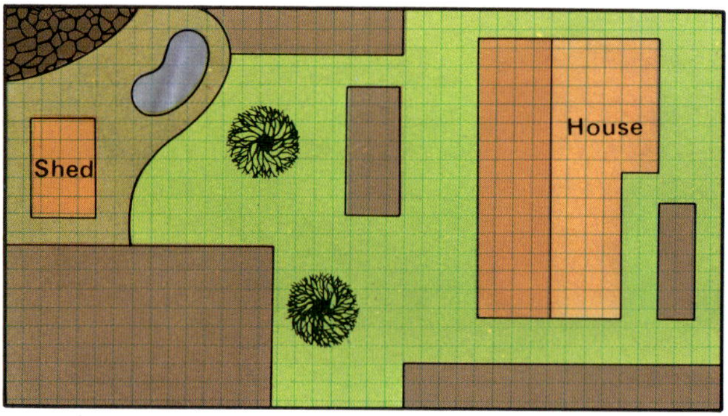

▼ Garden planning means making the best of the available space, and if there are undesirable features, hiding or adapting them carefully.

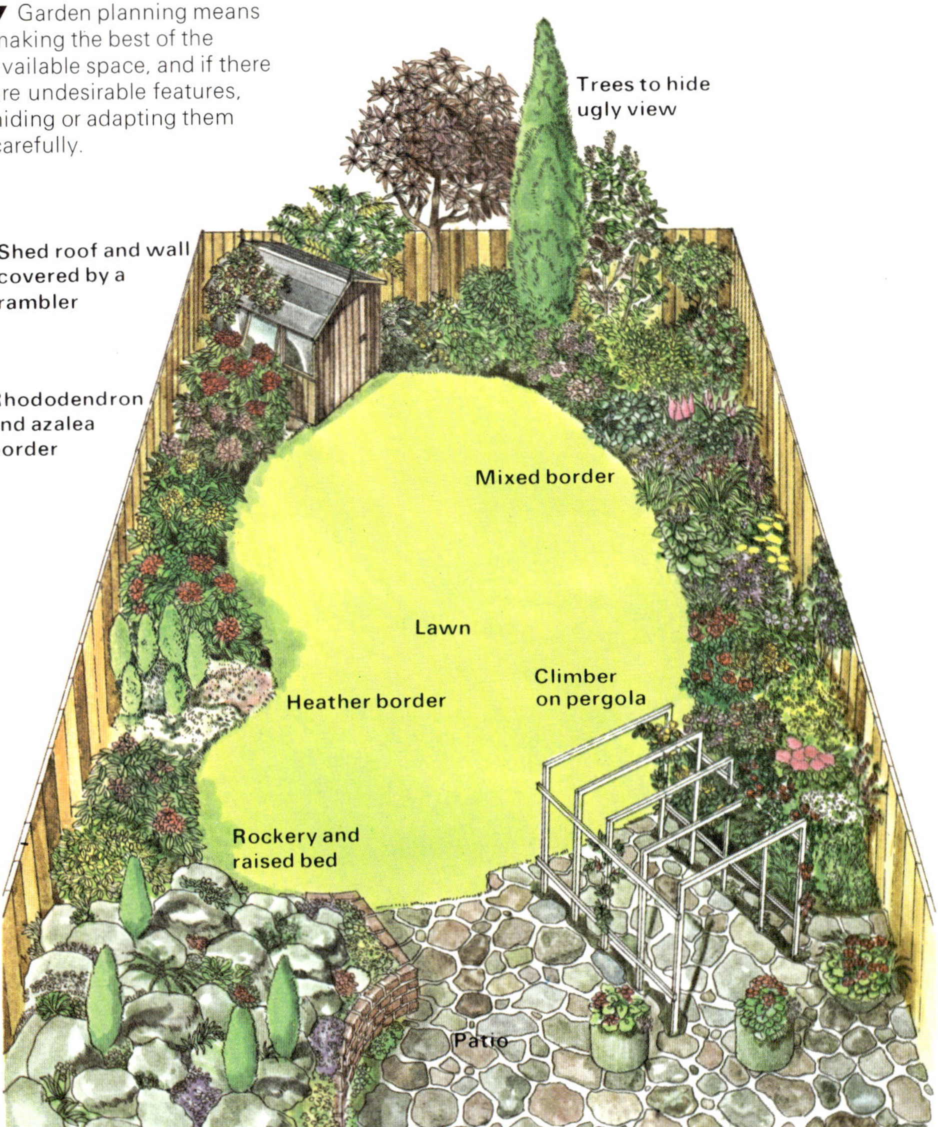

that they should not be planted too close together, or close to paths, fences or the house, where in a few years time they would prove a nuisance. Remember too that tree roots can damage house foundations, and may enter the joints in sewage or surface-water drains and cause blockages. Make sure that you find the position of pipes and underground or overhead cables, and avoid them in case of any future repair work. You can determine the route of underground services by drawing a straight line between manhole covers on your own and neighbouring gardens.

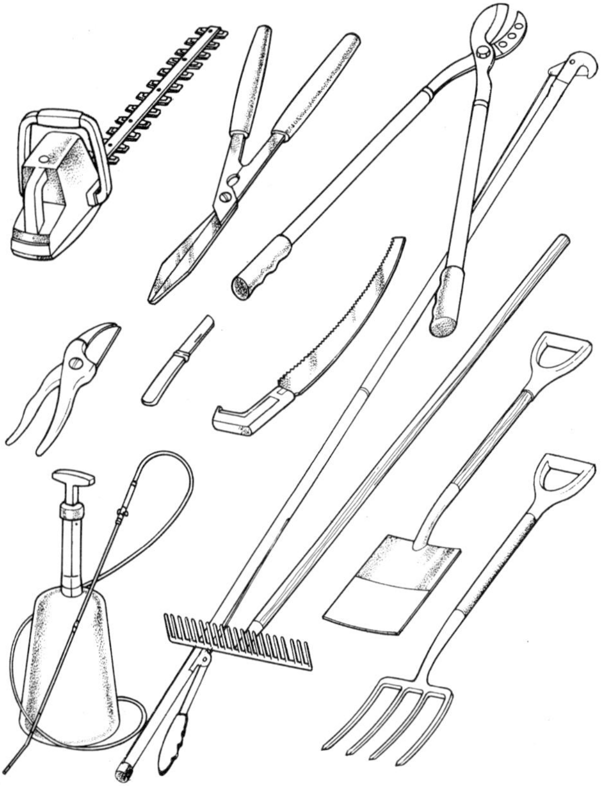

Tools

To plant and maintain your trees and shrubs you will need all the normal garden tools, plus a few more specialized pieces of equipment to cater for the extra size and robust growth of these plants. Spade, fork and rake are all essential; not a small lightweight spade or fork though, as you will need to dig deep and probably will have to shift a fair amount of soil in the early planting stages.

A sprayer is very useful for applying insecticides and fungicides. The ordinary 'flit-spray' hand type is not adequate. Far better is the kind with a reservoir, which can be slung from the shoulder, containing 4 to 5 litres of mixture which is applied from the hand-held gun.

Heavy shears and pruning shears are indispensible. Trying to improvise with ordinary secateurs will lead to split or damaged branches and a risk of fungal disease. For shaping larger trees, use a special pruning saw, which usually folds safely away like a large penknife. Look after all these tools. They have to work hard on the larger trees and shrubs and are expensive to replace if damaged by rust and neglect.

Tools for hire

Many of the tools most useful for occasional heavy work, and especially for clearing overgrown or neglected gardens, can be hired at reasonable cost. A rotary power cultivator is ideal for clearing large areas and a flame gun makes light work of weeds and their seeds. A chain saw will cut up an old tree in an hour or so. And for fiddly but important jobs such as digging deep, narrow, post holes for a fence, hire a soil auger.

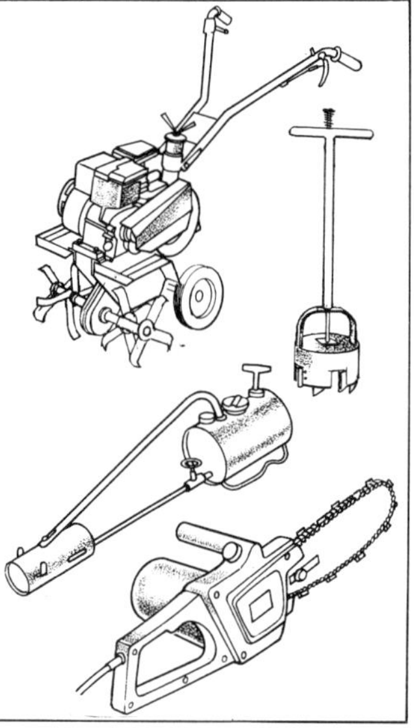

Digging

Digging is the preliminary stage in planting your new tree or shrub. You may have an established garden, in which case you have only to prepare the ground im-

▲ Single digging

▼ Double digging

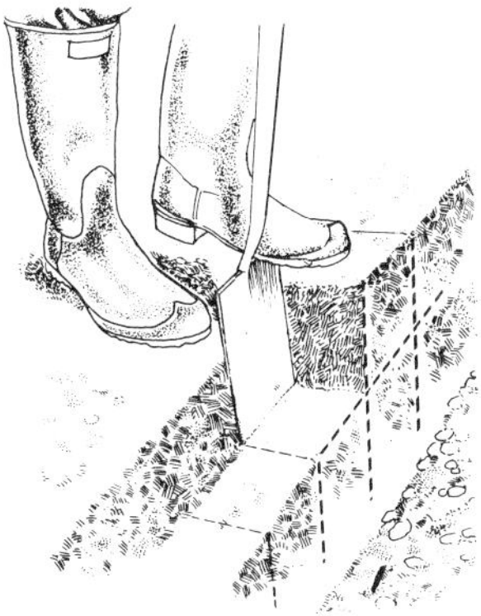

mediately round the planting area. If your garden has been neglected for a long while, or is on a new property with builders' rubble and clay strewn about, your problem is greater.

Remove all stumps, lumps of stone or concrete, and large pieces of hard clay. You will have to arrange their disposal in a public waste tip. Ideally you should begin soil preparation in autumn or early winter, so that frost and rain will help to break up lumps of soil.

Use the largest spade you can manage unless the ground is very hard, in which case a fork will be easier. And use your body weight rather than shoulders and arms to force the spade into the ground, turning the soil over one spadeful or spit at a time in a neat row. Then start at the same end and dig another row, and so on, until the bed is completely dug. Break up the lumps with hoe and rake to produce a fine tilth. If your garden has been regularly cultivated, this is sufficient preparation, but if the ground is in bad condition, double digging may be necessary—a much tougher proposition. In this technique the first spit is removed, then a further spit is taken from the bottom of the trench, breaking into undisturbed sub-soil. This sub-soil is usually very hard-packed, but it is possible to take a short-cut by simply breaking it with a fork rather than turning the second spit over. Whichever method you use, take the opportunity to work in any manure or soil treatment you may require. Although not actually a plant food, peat is always worth adding as it improves the soil texture enormously.

Soil testing

The degree of acidity or alkalinity (pH) is most important. In general, peat soils are acid while chalky soils are alkaline. If in doubt about the type of soil you have, a soil test kit will allow you to determine the pH value. A neutral pH around 7 suits most plants. If the figure is very high, work plenty of peat into the soil to neutralize excess alkalinity. If very low (4·5 to 5), either work in lime or cultivate only acid-loving shrubs.

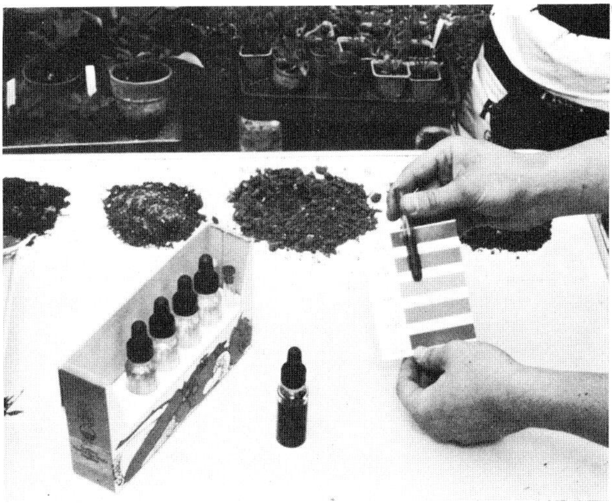

For decorative beds, levelling is not as important as for the vegetable garden, but you may wish to change the slope for aesthetic reasons. Use a string stretched between two pegs to give an accurate line and rake soil to give the slope you require. Bear in mind that as you shift soil from high spots, you will be reducing the depth of the area you have already prepared. It will probably be necessary to re-dig such areas, if the subsoil has been exposed or is near the surface.

Arranging the plants

Use of shrubs in a garden demands a certain amount of planning and imagination. Too many of the wrong type can produce the sort of gloomy shrubberies which still persist in parks laid out at the beginning of this century. To produce their best, both trees and shrubs must be integrated with the garden as a whole. Many shrubs are grown purely for the beauty of their flowers. Unfortunately, they have definite growing seasons; most flower in spring, and the rest continue throughout the summer. If you wish to grow many flowering shrubs or trees, you will have to decide on the flowering characteristics and colouring of each, in order to plan a harmonious display which will always present you with some colour.

Using the reference section in this book, or other sources, you must find the ultimate height and spread of each shrub or tree you plant, and take this into account when planting them. Although smaller shrubs can be moved in their dormant season over the winter if an error in planning is made, such a move is best avoided by a little forethought. If your plan includes slow-growing specimens, however, it may be worth including rapidly-growing and cheap shrubs such as forsythia, buddleia, or cytisus, which can be dug out when their choicer neighbours have developed to a better size and need the space.

Because shrubs, and to a lesser extent trees, grow to every conceivable shape, from slim and erect down to creeping or prostrate forms, they can be made to blend with any kind of herbaceous plant. Their obvious use is as a background behind clumps of bulbs, annuals, or herbaceous perennials, but because there are so many tiny dwarfed forms, do not overlook the possibility of using trees or shrubs at the front

▶ The truly informal mixed bed has a well-thought-out blend of herbaceous perennials, annuals and shrubs and trees which can give flower for most of the year.

BEDDING SCHEMES

▶ Large shrubs (**1**) form a background to more compact shrubs (**2**) while in the foreground is a solid bed of small herbaceous flowering plants (**3**).

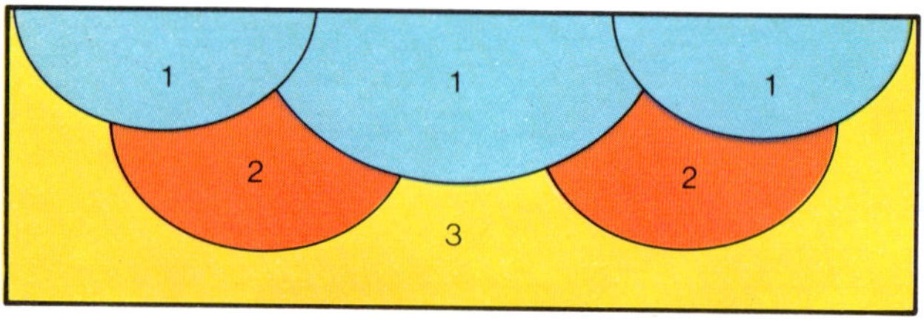

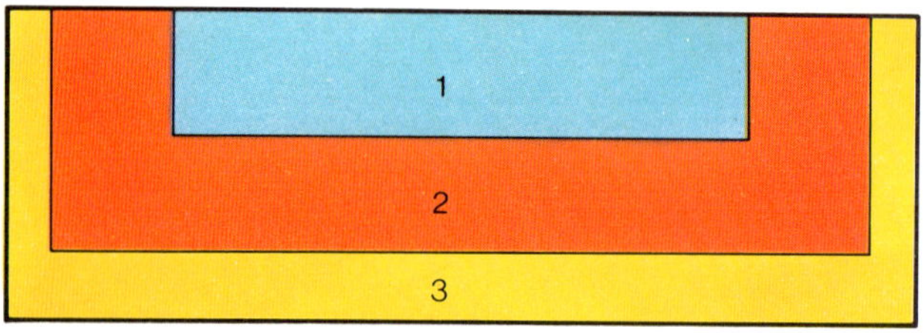

◀ This more formal bed still depends on the same principles as the scheme above. Large shrubs are grouped together to form a background to smaller herbaceous plants in front.

of the bed, perhaps to divide the clumps of herbaceous plants. Similarly, a few, tall, slim trees can be planted among some low-growing flowers, and because of their shape, will not hide either these or plants growing towards the back of the bed.

Do not neglect the subtler aspects of shrubs and trees. Some may be a perfect foil for the brilliant range of colours of annual flowers—the soft greys and blues of conifers, for example. Remember also the variations in leaf colour and the shapes and sizes of leaves. Use of a reasonable number of shrubs in a mixed border adds stability to your display. A border composed only of annuals will provide a brilliant show for a limited period, but will speedily become untidy and colourless after flowering, and will need complete replanting. However, a border well planted with shrubs and small trees is a thing of beauty in itself, and the naturally divided areas in which the short-lived annuals are grown are far more easily restocked, as well as looking more natural.

If your garden plan calls for an informal 'cottage garden' appearance, this apparently random pattern of shrubs and herbaceous plants will provide the beds you require. Always remember that taller plants should be at the back, apart from the occasional specimen in the centre of the beds. Do not forget too that herbaceous plants are frequently capable of growing as high as many of the shrubs; so some of these can also be planted towards the back of the bed. Delphinium, althaea, and lupins are typical herbaceous perennials which grow very tall, and are best treated like shrubs or small trees as far as garden planning is concerned.

For a semi-formal appearance, plants are arranged more neatly. To obtain beds with this kind of precise layout, you will need to buy large numbers of the same types of plant. These are not planted in rows, but enable large areas to be covered. This type of layout generally demands that larger shrubs are ranked towards the back of the bed, with lower-growing forms towards the front, so that a terraced appearance is obtained, even though the ground surface beneath is quite level.

In any type of mixed bedding plan, take into account the winter months when few if any plants will be flowering. Conifers and evergreens are then very useful. These will possibly be overshadowed in the spring and summer months, but their subtler colours and shapes come into their own when the flowers and foliage have died off on the other plants in the bed.

Shaped borders

For marking out shaped borders, you will need to refer to your garden plan (see page 16), on which you will have indicated the approximate size and shape of the beds. If you want to keep closely to your design, you must first mark out with string and pegs the main squares indicated, which you drew on graph paper. This time, the squares you lay out with string are full size, i.e. if your drawing is scaled at 1 cm:1 m, then make your string grid of 1 m squares. Having established where the beds or other features will be, you can mark in the curves using a pointed stick or a thin trickle of sand, ready for digging out later.

For an informal garden, this will produce reasonably accurate curves, but if circular or oval beds are needed, a different technique for marking out must be used. Mark out a circular bed by driving a stake in the central point and scribing a circle round it with another sharpened stake tied to a string of

▼ As with other bedding schemes, the island bed demands careful siting of the individual shrubs. A few large central specimens are set off by the lower-growing plants spread round them.

▶ Curved borders preserve the informal appearance of these beds. The terracing, using paving stones between the levels, helps to stop the soil slumping after heavy rain.

the correct radius. Ovals are more difficult. Drive in two widely separated guide stakes, then spread your string loosely around them in a loop. Move your marker stake round this loop, pulling the string taut, and it will scribe an oval. You will probably have to move the central pegs and vary the length of the loop to make the size and shape you need.

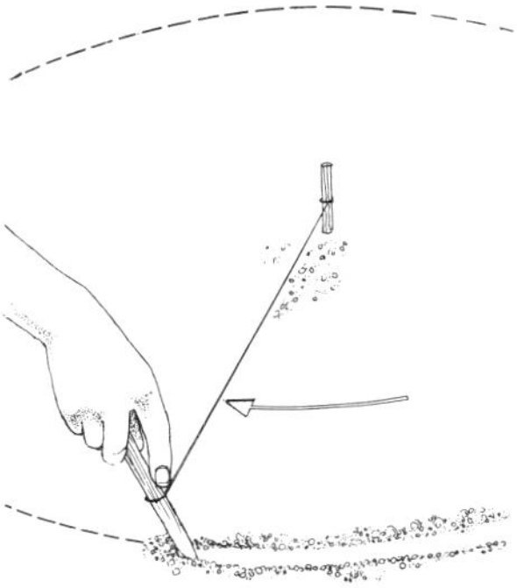

Planning the rose bed

Like beds for any other plant, the rose bed must be prepared and dug thoroughly, after being marked out in accordance with your garden plan. But unlike many other shrubs, roses demand special soil conditions if they are to thrive.

The selected site for your rose bed must be in as sunny a spot as possible. Too much shade, and fungal diseases and poor flowering are inevitable. Your bed must be thoroughly double-dug (see page 19) and as much organic material as possible worked into the lower spit. This can be peat, sawdust, seaweed, straw, chopped up turf, material from your compost heap, or even balls of newspaper—in fact, anything which is capable of rotting down. In the top spit, use well-rotted compost, peat or leaf-mould, with a liberal sprinkling of bone-meal. If your soil is heavy and full of clay, work sand, gravel, or well-weathered clinker into the spits to improve drainage. Soil conditioners based on seaweed compost are available which do a remarkable job of breaking up clay lumps without digging, and these will also help improve the soil in your rose bed. Roses prefer slightly acid soil, so if your soil is too chalky, use plenty of peat to improve the acid balance. If it is strongly acid, a sprinkling of lime will help neutralize the excess. If in doubt, use a test kit to determine the degree of acidity or alkalinity in your soil.

Climbers and trellises

Many climbing shrubs will grow well over an already existing feature in the garden, such as an old stump or a wall. However, if you have planned your ideal garden, you may wish to dictate where climbing features should be situated, and in this case, trellises or other constructions are a convenient form of support. Trellises can be bought ready-made in standard sizes, or may be made very easily from wood strips, fixed together with galvanized nails to stop cor-

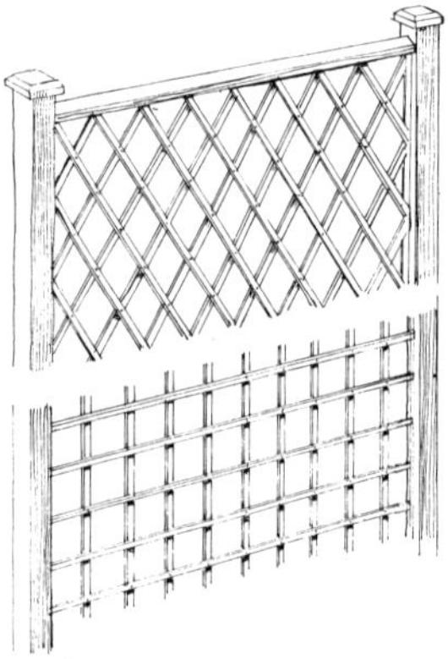

rosion. If the wood is untreated, or if you make your own trellis, it will need rot-proofing. Do not use creosote. It may be cheap, but it will certainly kill any plant it touches, until at least a year after first being applied. There are several proprietary rot-proofing agents containing copper preservatives which can be purchased at your local garden centre.

Pergolas

The pergola is an old-fashioned garden feature enjoying a comeback. It consists of a heavy wooden frame, with cross-pieces

forming an openwork tunnel, round which climbers can be trained. These used to be built along the length of a path and vines, wisteria and other large climbers were grown over them. In today's smaller gardens, they are less grand affairs, but can be used to good effect on a patio. The pergola is rather expensive to construct, needing timbers at least 12cm square for the uprights and cross-pieces secured together with coach-bolts. They can be treated with rot-proofer and left in their natural wood finish, or painted white if prefered. A heavily overgrown pergola casts a considerable amount of shade, so care must be taken in their positioning and in the choice of plants for them.

Arches

If your garden is large enough to have separate sections for vegetables and leisure areas, a decorative arch is a useful feature to help screen off the less attractive parts. Ready-made arches can be purchased in wood or in plastic covered metal which needs no maintenance. They can also be built very easily, using the same materials as trellises. Use some thought as to the plants you will grow over the arch. Climbing roses are very much in keeping with the country garden image many people strive for, but

are not very practical to walk through when the arch becomes overgrown.

Rustic poles

Shrubs which are too heavy for trellises can be grown along and up very simple constructions of poles with the bark left in place. These rustic pole frames are usually short-lived, as they cannot be effectively rot-proofed, but are cheap to make if you have ready access to fresh-cut timber.

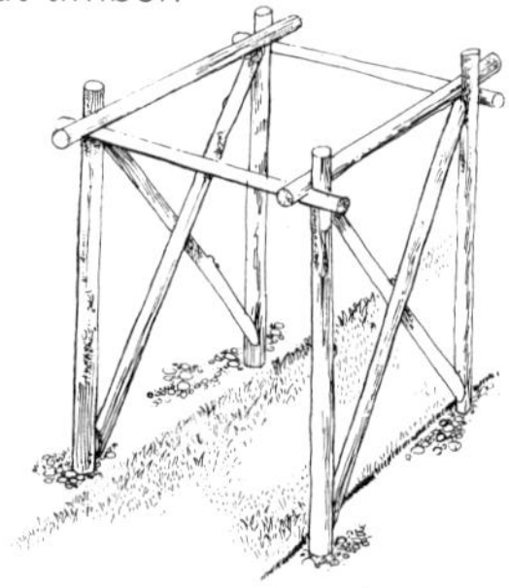

Selecting plants

Selection and purchasing of trees and shrubs has been made much easier in recent years with the advent of the garden centre—a gardener's supermarket where a wide range of plants is displayed. The other factor which has helped the gardener immeasurably is the introduction on a very large scale of container-grown plants.

Container-grown plants

Trees and shrubs can be grown in tubs, plastic containers, or even in flimsy plastic sheet 'pots', and this has a number of advantages over the traditional nursery where trees and shrubs are planted directly into the ground. The container-grown plant can be purchased and moved at any time of year—even in its flowering season. Because its roots have been restricted by the container, they will be compact and this makes planting much easier than the straggly roots found on most plants grown directly in the soil. But they also have the important disadvantage of being expensive, because they demand more handling and attention from the nurseryman. Buy container-grown plants for instant effect, but if you want large or unusual plants, go to a specialist nursery where the stock is grown in the open ground. Because garden centres must obtain container-grown stock from many specialist sources, they will usually only stock the commonest or most popular types.

▲ Large choice specimens can be selected at any time of year from a specialist tree nursery. Usually they will be delivered in late autumn.

Specialist nurseries

Specialist nurseries will have a better selection of plants from which to choose, and you will also find large specimen trees here. If you buy from these sources, either by going personally to the nursery, or by ordering from a catalogue, you will have to wait until late autumn before you can take delivery of your purchases, when growth has stopped and leaves have fallen from deciduous plants. The advantages of this are that the nurseryman, who does not want you complaining that

your new stock has died, will choose the best and safest time to ship the plants, usually with the roots bare of earth. In this way, quite large trees can be bought as well as smaller shrubs such as roses, which are usually supplied not only bare-rooted, but also thoroughly pruned.

Points to consider

Your selection of shrubs and trees must take two factors into account. First, make sure you are buying the right plants for the job, and second, make sure the specimens you purchase are healthy. There is no point in planting a large tree such as a cedar or weeping willow on a small front lawn if you are going to have to dig up the tree together with most of the lawn in a few years when it has outgrown its position. If you really like that type of tree, look through the catalogues and find a dwarf or slow-growing variety. Similarly, if you live in an area where the soil is heavy and alkaline, consider whether it is worth even trying to grow rhododendrons and azaleas. They will grow, certainly, but will be straggly and sickly. To keep them in good health would demand frequent applications of extremely expensive sequestered iron. It is much cheaper to grow something different.

Purchase of trees and shrubs is similarly a matter for commonsense. Most plants that are diseased look sickly. The points to watch out for are discoloured leaves, insect pests and scorching or dying-back (this is particularly obvious on the buds and shoot tips). Always try to select a large and well-shaped plant—not necessarily the tallest. Instead, look out for a bushy specimen with plenty of side-shoots, which will keep its shape as it grows. Give some thought also as to how you will get your purchases home. Trees and shrubs are difficult to get into a car, and almost inevitably shoots will be broken and buds knocked off. It is better to pay a small additional charge and have them delivered in perfect condition by the nursery.

Planting

Planting is the most critical time for any tree or shrub. Any mistakes you make now may be impossible to rectify later without digging up the plant and causing setbacks in growth. Correct planting will make all the difference between a sickly plant, slow to begin healthy growth, and one which will grow vigorously right from the beginning.

Bare rooted shrubs and trees

Your new stock will probably arrive from the nursery at any time after late autumn, when virtually all growth has stopped. There is no point in planting if the weather is very bad—wet and windy—or if it is too dry to allow the roots to 'take', for they will grow a small amount even in the dormant period during the winter.

It is usual to 'heel in' new trees and shrubs until you are ready to plant them properly. This involves simply digging a trench one spit in depth, into which the newly arrived plants are laid at an angle to prevent wind damage. Remove root wrappings and spread the roots over the bottom of the trench so the plant will be able to stand up securely against winter gales. If the branches are tied up to make the plant more compact during transport, untie the fastenings and spread the branches out to recover their normal shape. Now cover the roots with soil and firm down with the foot—the 'heeling-in' process.

Soil preparation

This is your last chance to

alter or improve the soil which will shortly be below the roots of your new trees and shrubs. Assuming you have either an established garden with reasonable soil,

or have prepared previously unsuitable ground by thorough double digging, now you must dig the actual planting hole. For even a smallish shrub, you will need to dig a hole about 60cm square, and one to two spits in depth. Break up the soil in the bottom of the hole with your fork, and sprinkle

in a couple of handfuls of bone-meal or similarly use proprietary fertilizer, together with a similar amount of compost, peat, or leaf-mould. Mix all this together thoroughly. Try to plant your trees and shrubs during a warm spell of weather.

Planting

Remove your plants from their temporary bed and stand each one in its planting hole. Spread the roots out carefully and prune off any which are broken or

withered, dusting the cut root-stump with charcoal, if possible. If your plant is going to need staking, now is the time to insert the stake to avoid root damage later. You must adjust the soil level at the bottom of the hole so that the original soil level round the plant (shown by the ring of dirt or discoloration on the stem) is exactly level with the soil in which you are planting it. This can be done by sifting top soil into the hole over the roots and lifting the plant slightly, allowing the soil to work down beneath the roots. Firm this soil down well, then add more top soil supporting the plant vertically as you do so. Do not fill the hole completely; add small amounts and firm down each time with the hands or a foot. Eventually the soil level round the new plant should be about 5cm above the surrounding soil level. This allows for later soil sinkage. Make a small cup-shaped depression round the stem to channel rainwater straight to the roots—your new plants' greatest need for a while is going to be water. If the ground is very dry a sprinkling is no good—what they need is a hose left running on the soil round the stem until the water ceases to soak in. It will then penetrate down to the roots.

Winter winds can cause excessive evaporation so conifers and evergreens will need protection against scorching and wilting.

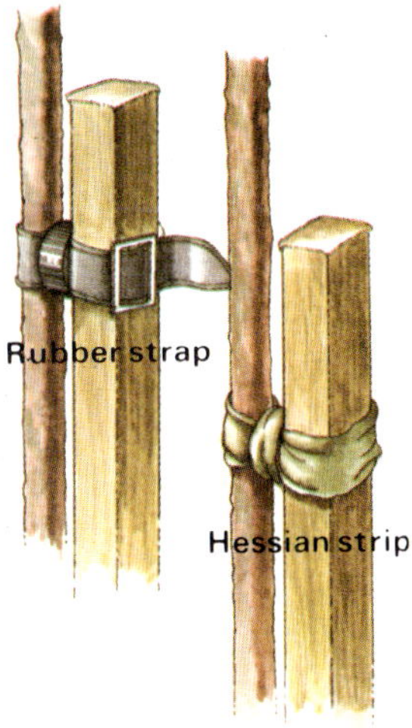

Staking

Winter winds are the chief cause of physical damage. Stems or branches can be snapped off and even worse is the loosening effect of continual rocking in the soil due to wind disturbance, which eventually ruptures supporting roots and allows the plant to be blown right over. With all young trees and some tall, spindly shrubs, staking is a necessity until the trunk or stems are at least 7cm in diameter—preferably even thicker.

With bare-rooted or container-grown trees or shrubs, staking must be carried out before the planting hole is filled, to avoid root damage as the stake is driven home at least 30cm below the base. Bear in mind that the plant is going to grow, so you will need a stake that at first will look much too large. It is also better to buy stakes pre-treated with preservative rather than make your own. Place the stake 8 to 10cm from the trunk or stem and use proprietary ties made of rubber or plastic to hold the plant firmly. Do not allow it to touch the stake, or wind movement will soon rub through the bark and allow fungus spores to enter.

Container-grown plants

When you buy container-grown plants, the season of the year is no longer important. You will need to prepare a planting hole in the same way as for bare-rooted plants and to make provision for staking, if necessary. If your plant is in a

rigid container or large pot, it can be knocked out by giving a sharp blow to the edge of the container while supporting the plant by its stem. The pot will come away leaving the soil-ball intact. If the plant has been grown in a bituminized-paper or flexible plastic container, this can simply be cut away.

Fill the hole gradually, as before, tamping the soil down well. Water thoroughly. If you are transplanting larger trees or shrubs from another site in your garden, the technique is just the same, it being important to preserve the soil-ball about the roots as much as possible.

In tubs and against walls

Any tree or shrub planted against a wall has to contend with half the normal root spread. It is denied adequate ventilation and will be more prone to fungal disease such as mildew. Yet another hazard is drips from a roof or gutter which may keep the foliage too damp. Before you plant any tree especially in such a spot, make very sure it cannot damage the

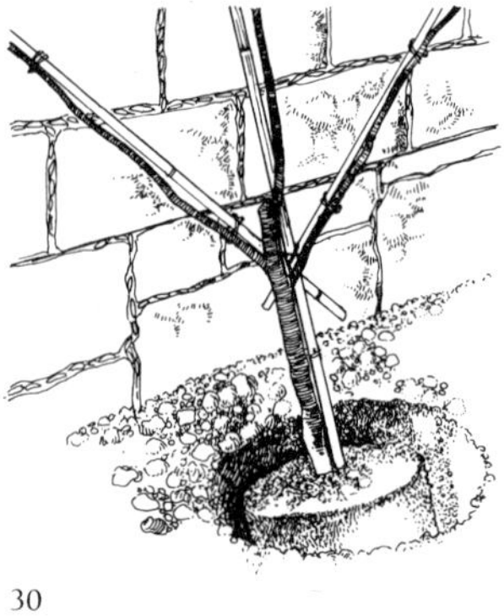

foundations of your home, by either root invasion or by drying out the soil enough to cause shifting and cracking in the walls.

Planting techniques are the same as for trees and

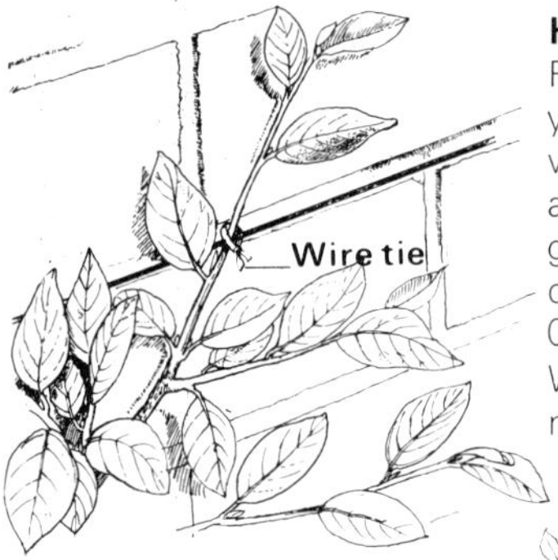

shrubs in open ground, except that staking is not necessary as the plant can be secured to the wall.

It is generally safer and more convenient to plant trees and shrubs in tubs so they can be stood against a wall or moved to a more exposed position. Planting in tubs entails the same care and precautions necessary elsewhere, particularly in re-

spect of added compost and fertilizers. The plants will need frequent feeding and for this reason, always use a disproportionately large tub to allow adequate root growth.

Hedges

First decide on the line of your hedge and mark it out with string, or if curved, drag a sharp stake along the ground. Prepare the site by digging one spit deep and 0·5m either side of the line. Work in the usual peat, leaf-mould or other compost,

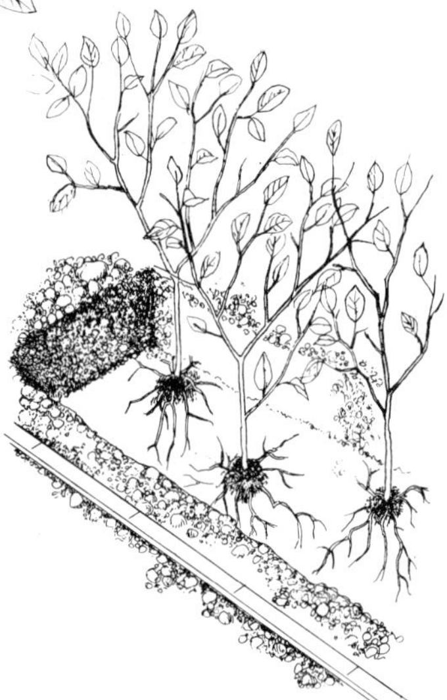

together with some fertilizer. The planting distance between your hedging plants will depend on the type you choose. For most plants, such as berberis and crataegus, about 45cm apart in a single row is sufficient. If you are going to plant trees which will be kept down to size by pruning, such as the beech (fagus) or holly (ilex), plant at 60-cm intervals. More spindly plants such as privet (ligustrum) need planting in a double row, with each plant staggered to provide a denser and thicker hedge.

Support your young hedging plants with a wire or wires stretched tightly along the hedge, clipping each plant to the wire with a tie. But remember the wire is there later on when the mature hedge needs clipping.

Planting roses

Roses are almost always delivered or supplied in a bare-rooted state in late autumn, and should be planted while the soil is still fairly warm. Soak them in a bucket of water for an hour, then heel them in until the bed can be properly prepared. Dig a hole one spit deep and about 30cm square, and dig a mixture of bone-meal and peat into the bottom. Trim off any remaining leaves or flowers, together with twiggy side-shoots. Plant the rose as any other shrub, filling the

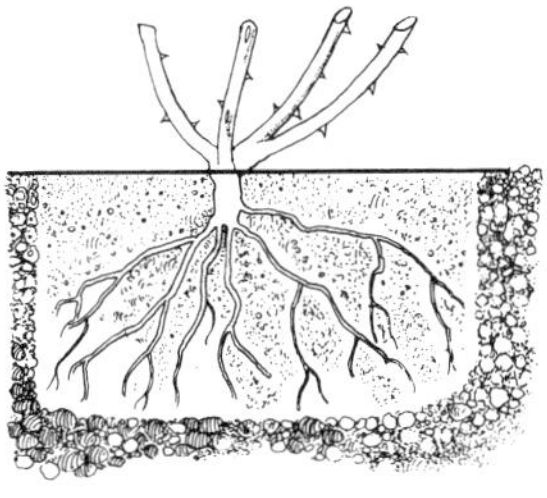

hole with a planting mixture of peat and bone-meal and firming down. Take great care to plant to the correct depth. The point where the green stems leave the brown rootstock must be

4cm beneath the ground surface. If they are planted too shallow this can encourage the development of suckers which will later ruin the plant. Similarly, with standard roses, use the old soil mark on the stem

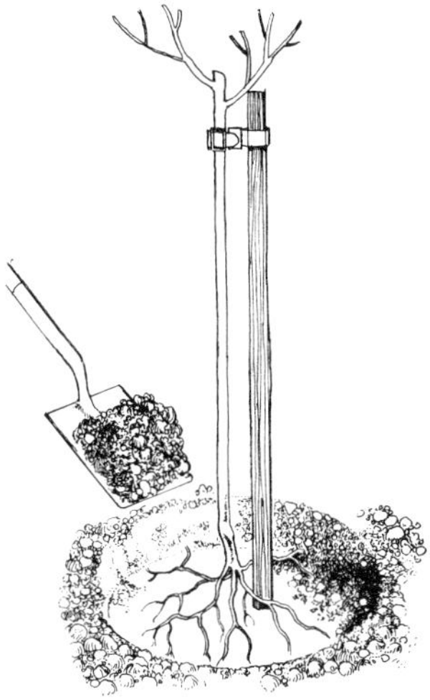

as a guide to planting depth. Stake them securely. Standards are an artificial plant to some extent, and are completely unable to withstand wind, being both brittle and shallow-rooted. Use two or more ties to secure them to the stake at several points along their stem. Walls are sometimes dry below ground, and for this reason, ramblers and

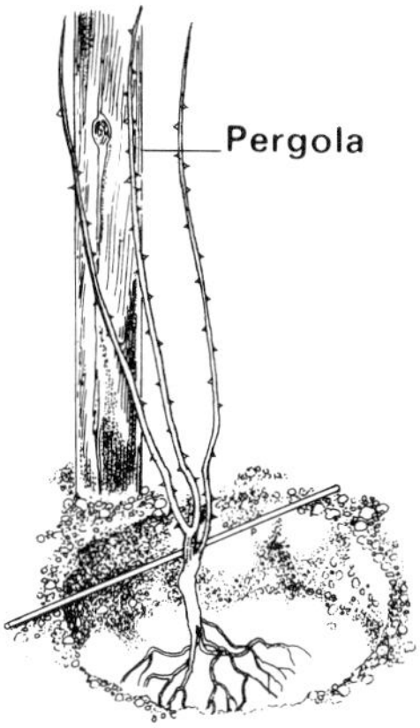

climbers should be planted at least 40cm out and trained back against their supporting wires or trellis. If they are able to grow up poles or a pergola, keep the roots at least 30cm from the base.

Maintenance

Compared to herbaceous plants, the woody-stemmed trees and shrubs need little routine maintenance, other than commonsense measures. They are less liable to be overwhelmed by neighbouring plants and are generally disease-resistant. The main problems they present are related to their size, which makes them liable to wind damage, and to 'taking over' part of the garden in an undesirable way, unless they are kept well under control by careful pruning and shaping.

Watering

Trees and shrubs use an enormous amount of water—more than could be supplied by hose in a large specimen. However, the plant sends down roots to a considerable depth where there is always an adequate amount of water, so the established tree or shrub seldom needs help from the hose. The newly planted tree or shrub, however, is very vulnerable and needs frequent watering until its roots are well established, which can take a couple of years. Always soak the ground thoroughly. Light watering encourages roots to spread near the surface, where they will be vulnerable to drought.

Weeding

Once a tree or shrub is well-established, weeds will be unable to rob it of a significant amount of nutrients or water. It is usual to leave a bare circle of at least 20-cm radius round any specimen planted in a lawn. This is for aesthetic reasons and to avoid stem damage from the mower, as the plant will not be affected by the growth of grass. Remove weeds in the usual way by hoeing, raking or hand weeding, but be very careful when hoeing near any tree or shrub. It is easy to nick roots or stems with the hoe, and therefore allow disease spores to enter. Similarly, be careful when hoeing round shallow, fibrous roots such as those of

rhododendrons, which are easily damaged. Although herbicides are good things to avoid, many gardeners use paraquat to kill weeds near woody-stemmed trees and shrubs, and use growth inhibitors such as simazine on rose beds to prevent the emergence of weeds.

Garden sprays

Like herbicides, insecticides and fungicides are chemicals which are best avoided, unless strictly necessary, because of the possibility of ecological damage to your garden. They do have their uses, however, and are safe to use if the instructions are followed correctly—they are of no use if they are applied carelessly. This means using a large sprayer capable of coating the whole plant with a film of chemical, not just the lower branches. Be especially careful to spray the underside of leaves, the growing tips and all buds, even those on minor side shoots. These are all protected spots where pests will cluster. Large pressure sprayers suitable for shrubs and trees have an extended lance which allows you to reach high branches. The intensity of the spray can also be varied to make sure that liquid penetrates to inaccessible spots in buds and in crevices in bark.

Feeding and mulching

Trees and shrubs are very tough, and have extensive root systems capable of spreading considerable distances through the soil in search of nutrients. Most will live quite happily without any fertilizers at all, although quite often, when a plant refuses to flower or looks sickly, it will have exhausted some particular type of soil nutrient. By the use of mulches, feeding will seldom be necessary. A mulch is a layer of peat, straw, grass cuttings, or even sawdust, which is spread round the base of trees or shrubs. Its functions are various. The mulch reduces evaporation from the soil and helps keep the roots damp. It also suppresses weed growth, because it is too loosely-packed for weeds to root themselves in it. Finally, it rots down and provides a continuous source of nutrients. Add other fertilizers if necessary by hoeing them in lightly, taking care not to disturb the roots.

▲ Mulching consists of spreading a layer of organic material on the soil surface. This keeps the soil moist and warm and, as the material rots, provides added nutrients to encourage root growth.

Foliar feeding

A comparatively new technique of feeding is the use of foliage sprays containing essential nutrients, plus some trace elements which are not usually included in other proprietary fertilizers. These are sprayed on in the same way as pesticides. They can have a dramatic effect on growth rate and colouring of a shrub, but they are very expensive to use on this scale, so their use is not likely to become routine, except for treating especially choice specimens.

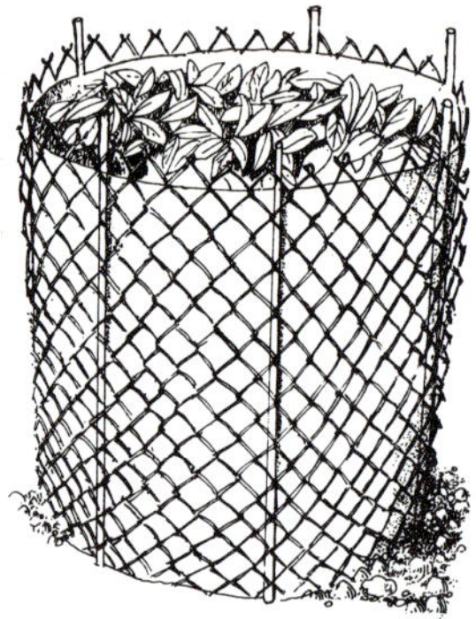

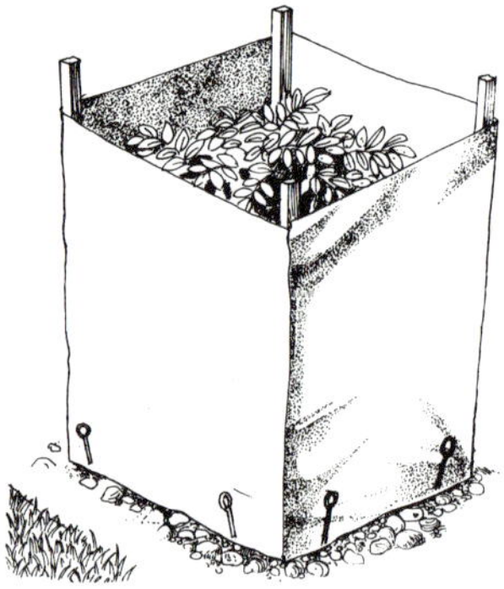

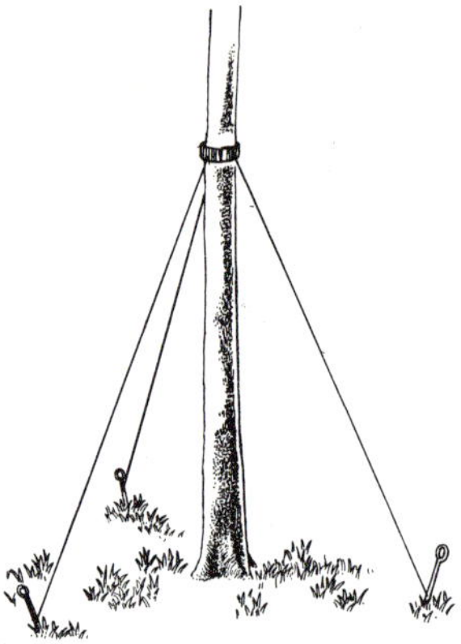

Frost protection

Frost damages trees and shrubs in various ways. Delicate trees will be scorched, and this is generally unavoidable, the dead tip growth being replaced each year by fresh shoots. Soil temperature is also important, and for shallow-rooted plants, such as rhododendrons, it is advisable to mulch thoroughly to a depth of at least 6cm before the first frosts. Evergreens are the most susceptible to frost damage, and the combination of cold winter winds and snow can cause irreparable damage.

Surround any vulnerable tree or shrub (this usually means newly-planted specimens) with a secure screen of plastic sheeting or sacking attached to stakes and covering as much of the plant as possible, leaving a ventilation space at the top. Peg the screen down to stop draughts getting underneath and chilling the ground. Smaller shrubs can be protected even better by packing straw or bracken down inside the screen.

Supporting

When a tree has outgrown its stake, it may still need supporting, especially if in an exposed position. Three wires braced to pegs can be used as a support, with the wires attached to a flexible collar round the trunk. This must be adjusted and loosened every year to avoid cutting into the bark. Large and also vulnerable branches can be supported in the same way, being braced to the trunk by wires attached to flexible collars.

Pruning, shaping and training

These three techniques are all used to force a tree or shrub to comply with the garden plan. At the same time, they can make the plant healthier and better able to resist weather and disease. Shaping is a crude technique, involving removal of large parts of the plant, such as overhanging branches, to change its general appearance. Pruning is the removal of limited parts of the plant, designed to force new growth which will be healthier or bushier than the previous growth. Training is the final step in the 'domestication' of a tree or shrub. It involves physically leading shoots and

branches into desired positions, which will eventually be 'frozen' as the woody content of the stems is laid down, making the plant more rigid.

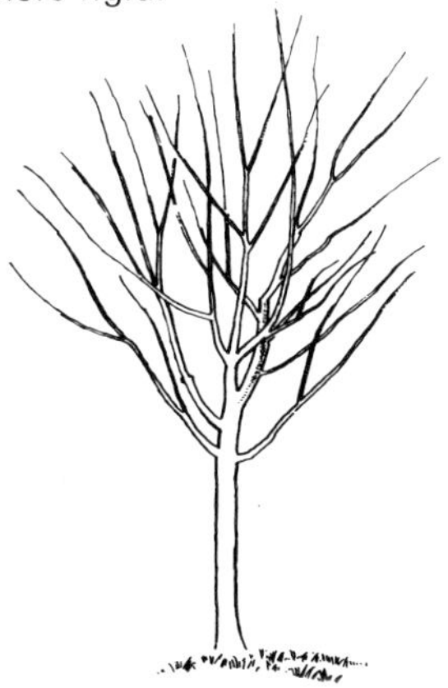

Shaping or removal of large branches demands some forethought if a tree is not to be permanently damaged. Be very sure that you really need to remove the branch, and consider whether such a removal might make the tree lop-sided. Make sure you have the right tools for the job. Branches up to 4cm in diameter can be cut with pruning shears, although large and expensive double-action cutters will be necessary for greater thicknesses. Use a hand saw for thicker branches to avoid splintering the wood. For very thick branches, a chain saw is the best solution.

The cutting technique is the same, whatever the size of the branch. First lop off the main part of the branch, at least 10cm away from the stem or trunk. If you are cutting a large tree branch, tie it to the main trunk with rope, to take the weight when the cut is complete. Cut from above, so the weight of the branch opens the sawcut, rather than causing it to grip the blade. If you wish you can first make a small cut on the underside of the branch nearer the trunk to prevent the bark tearing as the branch breaks away from the cut.

Now you must make the second cut to leave the trimmed branch tidily smoothed-off against the trunk. As there is no heavy

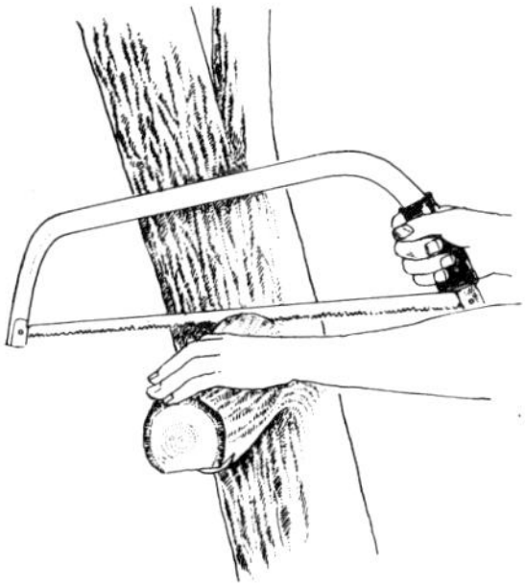

branch to cause tearing and splitting, or locking of the saw blade, you can cut from any convenient angle. The object is to trim away the stub of the branch so as to avoid unsightly stumps, yet not so close as to damage the living heartwood of the main trunk. Make your cut

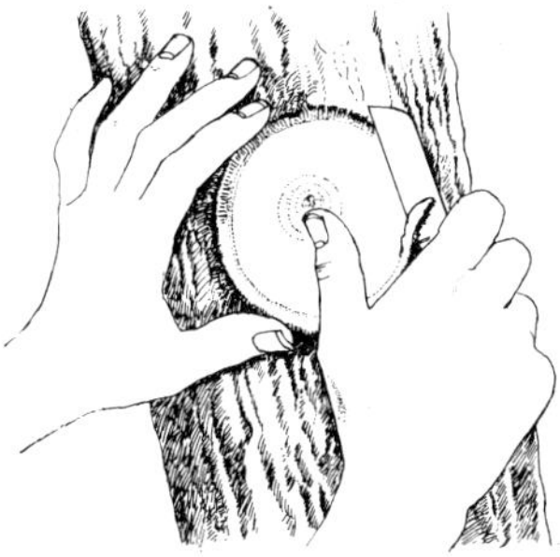

at a slight angle so that water is guided off from the scar. Use a sharp knife to

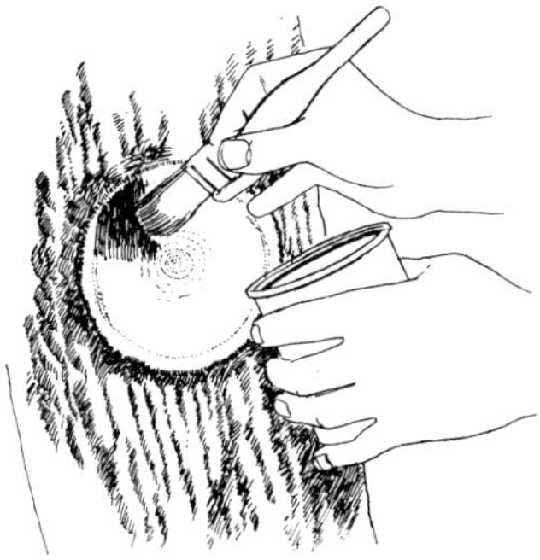

pare away jagged pieces of wood or bark, and round off the edges of the wound neatly. The wound will gradually heal over, but while this happens, it must be covered with a pruning-dressing.

Pruning shrubs

The techniques of pruning shrubs vary depending on the species. For more unusual varieties, it is wise to consult a specialist book on the subject. For the common fast-growing shrubs, however, the techniques are always similar, although you must find out if your shrub flowers on new growth, or the previous season's wood, before making drastic cuts. You must use your judgement and commonsense.

First locate any dead or damaged branches or stems, or any which look diseased. Cut them out cleanly with pruning shears, as close to their bases as possible, remembering to make a diagonal cut to allow rain run-off. Now look for suckers springing up from the roots. There are various good reasons for removing these. Many plants are grafted on to less attractive root stocks, and the suckers arising from these will spoil the appearance of the plant. Even if suckers are the same as the main plant, they will soon produce an untidy thicket. Symphoricarpus is particularly prone to this. Cut the suckers below the soil surface, if possible, to prevent regrowth.

Stand back and look at the general shape of the plant. Decide what size and shape you are aiming for and then prune away any unsightly branches, including those which are too tightly packed for good growth. Thin out untidy or spindly growth, particularly branches growing within the crown of the plant which are heavily shaded by the outer growth. By now, the main branches or stems which you will want to preserve should be obvious.

When to prune

Spring-flowering shrubs, such as forsythia and winter-flowering jasminum, bloom on shoots produced before the appearance of the leaves. These must therefore be pruned as soon as possible after flowering. Summer- and autumn-flowering shrubs must be pruned in their dormant season over the winter. As they produce flowers on new growth, it is obviously advantageous to cut them back hard in order to force them to produce as much new growth as possible. This can be done at any time over the winter, but is best saved for immediately before growth starts in the spring.

The simplest rule for pruning conifers is—don't. The beauty of most conifers lies in their perfect shape and pruning can only spoil them. The exceptions are prostrate forms such as trailing juniperus, which can have intrusive or badly positioned branches removed.

Broad-leaved evergreens similarly do not benefit from pruning, which leaves unsightly gaps in their tightly-packed foliage. Avoid pruning unless absolutely essential.

Pruning roses

All roses need pruning every year regardless of species or variety. And roses are so tough that it is very unlikely that even the severest pruning could harm them.

Rose pruning comes in two basic stages for the hybrid teas and the floribundas. First is winter pruning, which is undertaken when the first frosts wither remaining flower-buds. Cut the twiggy growth and top off the main stems at about 30 to 40cm from the soil level, depending upon the original size of the bush.

The second stage of pruning takes place in early spring, just before growth starts. The first objective is to remove all thin or straggly stems from the base of the plant so low down that no

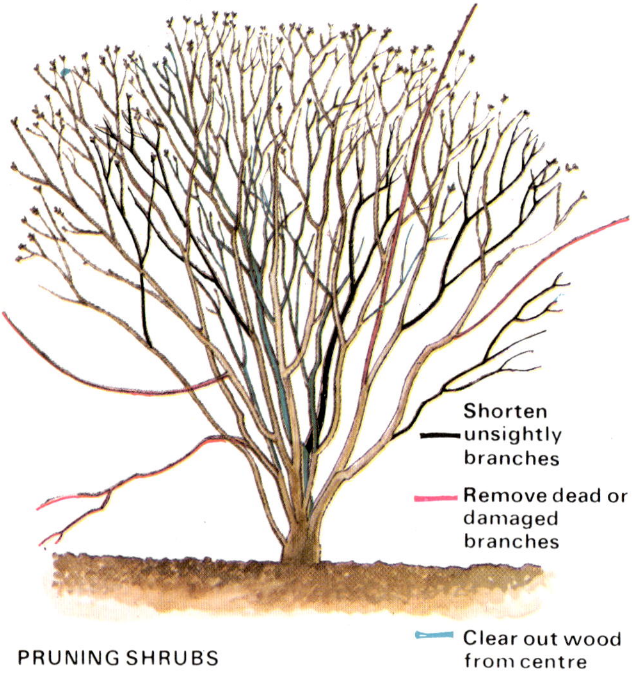

PRUNING SHRUBS

new growth can arise from dormant buds. These buds can be found as tiny pink specks, nestled in a scar on the stem. Cut very carefully to avoid splintering or tearing the stem. The remaining healthy stems, which will form the basis for the new year's growth, can now be pruned.

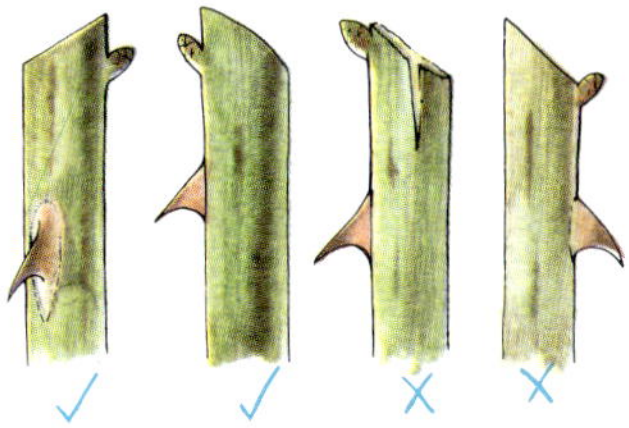

PRUNING ROSES

Opinions on the place to cut differ, but the following technique is widely used. Look at the base of each stem for the lowest bud facing outwards and make your cut above this. You may well find that this means the bush will be cut back almost to ground level, but this will not hurt it at all. Choosing this position means that the new growth will swell outwards, producing a well-shaped bush. However, if from previous years' experience you know that the rose has a sprawling growth, as sometimes happens with floribundas, pruning back to inward-facing buds will produce a more erect growth. The way in which the actual cut is made is critical. If you cut too close to the bud, die-back will cause the bud to wither, with the loss of a whole stem. The diagram on this page shows the precise position in which to make your cut. Any other will cause aborted buds and risk the entry of disease organisms.

Removal of suckers is very important, but do not mistake them for shoots growing from the base of the plant. These new shoots are important for the health of the rose and will produce the strong growth needed for healthy flowering. Suckers spring from the briar on which the rose is grafted, and their appearance is quite different. Usually they have many more thorns and a different leaf shape from the main plant. Scrape away the soil surface, and cut the sucker as close to its origin in the root as possible.

Throughout the flowering season, you may be pruning inadvertently when you cut blossom, so give some thought on the effect on the plant of removal of the flower, especially if you cut one with a long stem. Throughout the year, soft twiggy growth will be produced. If this growth does not have flower-buds and seems too soft to carry flowers, rub out the new growth with your thumb, or prune away carefully at its junction with a stronger stem, making sure you do not leave a bud from which more growth can start.

Training

The combination of pruning with physical restriction or redirection of growth allows you to train a tree or shrub into an unnatural shape. But the art of training is to make this artificial shape appear natural. Most garden trees, if left to their own devices, produce an untidy mass of growth which envelops the trunk from ground level up. The crown, or position at which most shoots arise, will be ill-defined and can

be at any height above ground. Training changes all this. Presuming you have started with a small tree, you must remove any side-shoots as they appear, usually by rubbing out the buds as they swell through

Half-standard

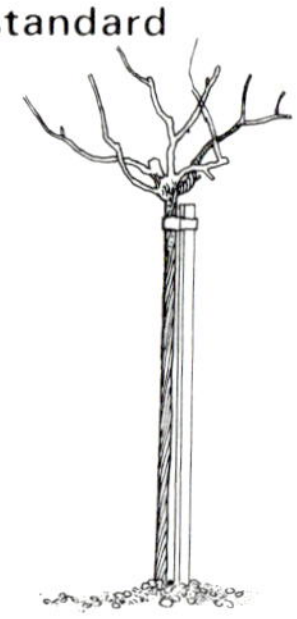

the bark. To encourage the tree to reach a good height, it will be necessary to select the shoot which will ultimately become the trunk, cutting out any secondary branches. The shoot you select will normally be one which is already growing in approximately the right position and is large and vigorous. This will be tied back to the stake to force it to grow vertically.

Horizontal trained

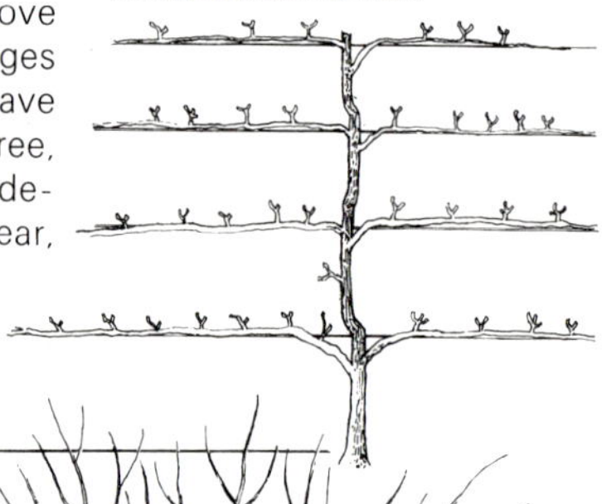

Standard

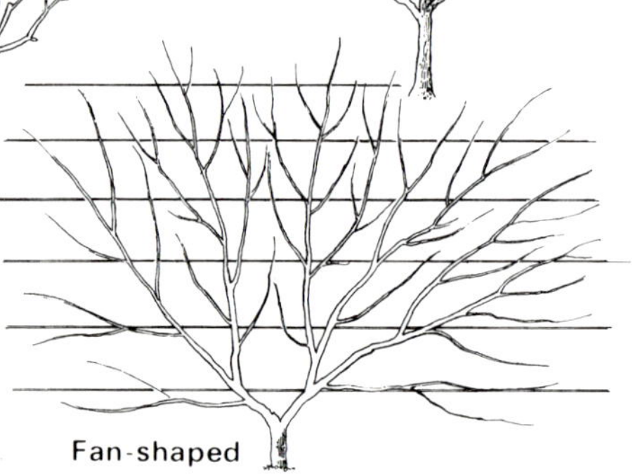

Fan-shaped

It is usual to train trees into either standard or half-standard form. This means trimming away side-shoots and encouraging vertical growth until the desired height is reached, at which point the tree is allowed to branch naturally. A standard tree usually begins to branch at about head height; a half-standard branches at about a metre above soil level.

Trees already part-grown can be forced to adopt these patterns by careful pruning and shaping. Sometimes the tree will run up too high before branching and then it is necessary to top it off, pruning out the centre shoot to force the plant to throw out branches. Similar techniques are used to produce wholly artificial shapes such as cordons, where the branches are trained to lie horizontally in the same plane, or fan-shapes, where they spread out at an angle also in the same plane. To produce trees with these forms, a supporting frame must be constructed to which the appropriate shoots are secured. This means constant attention throughout the growing season. Even a climber such as wisteria, which forms a heavy, woody stem, can be trained into an upright tree form, provided a very strong stake is used. This will produce a beautiful weeping tree, which flowers heavily. It is probably best grown in a tub which can be moved around to catch the sun.

Trees and shrubs grown

against walls need a certain amount of training. When a tree is grown against a wall, it needs securing and training to stop it rubbing against the masonry and to keep it clear of gutters and windows. Such problems can be avoided to some extent by planting self-clinging climbers, such as *Hydrangea petiolaris*, which demand the minimum of attention.

Some prostrate or trailing trees and shrubs need training to allow them to provide useful cover in the garden. Cotoneaster species with a prostrate habit make excellent cover for unsightly drain covers, but having stiff and springy stems, need pegging or staking, or hard pruning, to encourage them to grow in the required direction. Vertical shoots should be removed.

Juniperus and some other species of conifer have attractive prostrate forms. However, these are difficult to train without destroying the attractive regular shape. If they must be pruned, take shoots only from the outside of the plant, to avoid leaving unsightly holes which will not heal for a long while.

Climbers

Most climbers, unless self-clinging, will need some assistance, and careful training. Clematis, for example, is capable of supporting itself with a few turns of its tendrils about a framework. As some climbers send out random shoots (tendrils) in attempts to find more supports, it will be necessary to tuck these wandering shoots into the main mass of the plant or into the frame. Judicious pruning is also necessary to remove straggly or unproductive growth.

Hedges

A newly-planted hedge needs some careful pruning if it is to thrive. Prune and shape each individual plant as it grows. Do not aim for height; instead, prune in such a way that a low bushy growth results, which will soon fill out the profile of the hedge with dense growth. Frequent pruning will encourage branching and with this good start the growing hedge can be shaped to fit the profile you are seeking.

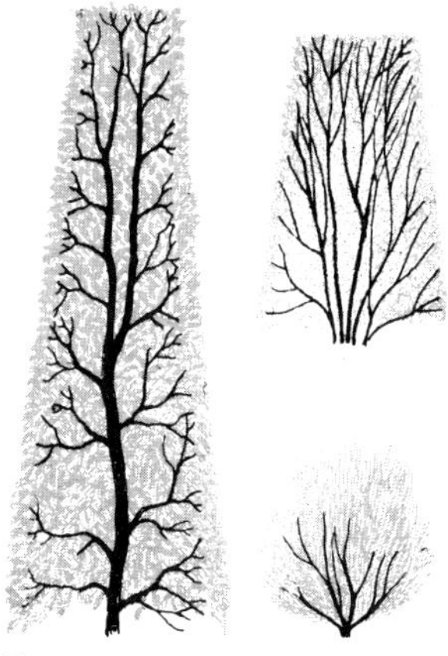

Roses

Climbers and ramblers need pruning and shaping just as do hybrid tea roses and floribundas. Most of these roses flower on the previous year's growth; that is, shoots which have not produced any flowers in the present year. The point of pruning is to remove growth which has already carried flowers and to preserve shoots which spring from ground level. So cut out any old stems just above where the new shoot appears.

These plants are vulnerable to wind damage; they

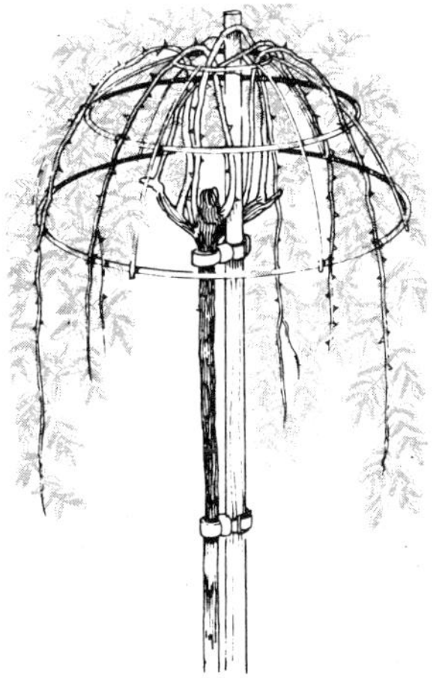

will need tying firmly to supports or to wire ties on a wall.

Weeping roses need special care. They take at least a year to become established and must be trained over an umbrella-shaped wire frame supported on a strong stake. Do not allow them to flower in the first year and pinch out any flower buds. Instead, encourage the growth of the strongest shoots, tying them firmly to the frame, and spreading them out so there are no unsightly gaps. As with other roses, prune away any twiggy growth. Subsequently you will be able to prune as for ordinary climbers or ramblers.

Special features

Shrubs and trees can be easily blended into a garden without altering the existing plan. But you might like to make a special feature of them which will highlight particular characteristics—colour, form or shape—or disguise an unwanted eyesore. Incorporating a rock garden, a hedge or raised beds, for example, need not necessarily mean drastic remodelling of the garden. However, some thought and effort is required so that features are correctly positioned to make the display most effective.

Natural features

It is possible to make special features which look natural, and can actually be quite natural. For example, if you live in an area where the ground is peaty, or which was formerly heathland, you will find it very easy to produce a heather garden, or to grow conifers and rhododendron; after all, these were some of the earliest plants growing here. If you already have a large number of good-sized trees you are well on the way to producing a small woodland

garden, with the minimum of work.

Creating new features

By taking into account your requirements, local soil conditions, climate and the material you have to work with, landscaping or re-contouring and other alterations in the appearance of your garden can be undertaken with confidence.

This need not involve earth-moving on the grand scale. Even the smallest garden is capable of supporting the growth of tiny dwarfed species of shrubs and trees, and the amount of re-modelling needed to provide suitable conditions for such plants is proportionately small. Remember too that trees and shrubs form only a part of the garden plan, and that changes can also involve paths, walls, patios and other structures which set off or decide the position for the plants. In some conditions it may be necessary or desirable literally to create a new landscape by shifting huge amounts of soil. It is never worth trying to do this by hand. Instead, try hiring a builders' digger for a few hours, or better still, find an obliging workman to do the job for you.

Attention to the soil

If you must shift soil on a large scale, do not forget that the soil you expose will not be fertile if it was formerly much more than 60cm beneath ground level. You will have to cover the exposed sub-soil with some of the top soil you shifted, or replace it with fresh soil brought in for the job. After such landscaping it will take years for the soil to settle fully. Trees planted on loosely packed soil slopes will often lean as the soil moves and settles, so try to plant only on the level. The roots of trees and shrubs will actually help to stabilize the newly-shaped soil.

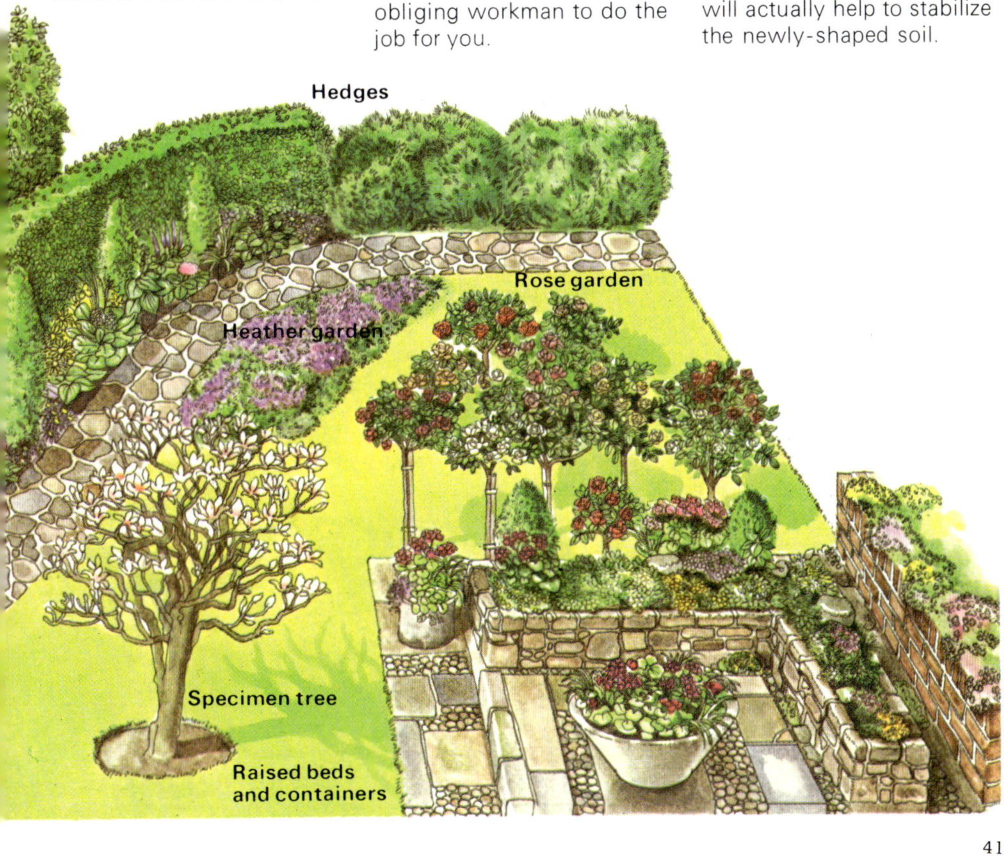

▶ The rock garden is a place where small plants can be grown without competition from their more rampant relatives. Conifers, heathers and a few rhododendrons are suitable species and care must be taken to select only true dwarf types. Plants which grow too large are very difficult to remove without damaging the structure of the rock garden. Construction is on the principle of the raised bed. A layer of ballast or hardcore provides drainage and the rocks, which must be attractively weathered, are cemented together to prevent slumping. Pockets of soil are left between them for planting.

RAISED BEDS

Raised beds are one of the simplest ways of creating a special feature in the small garden. They allow very small trees and shrubs to be planted in such a way that they are displayed quite close to the eye, yet cannot be swamped by the more vigorous growth of larger plants. They are particularly valuable as an edging to the patio or bordering a path. And, of course, you can use many other types of plant as well.

A raised bed can be built from a wide variety of materials. If you are lucky enough to live in an area where large slabs of stone are plentiful, use these to build a cavity wall. The space between the rows of slabs should be about 30cm and filled with soil in which the plants can be grown. The wall itself can be 'dry' if the stones are large enough, or else cemented like a brick wall. Exactly the same technique can be used to build a raised bed from bricks, preferably old, weathered ones, from a demolished building. The pressure of the earth is considerable and will cause the walls to bulge unless buttresses are built in every metre or so. Leave spaces between the bricks in odd places so that trailing plants can root in them and give the bed a more natural appearance.

The easiest type of raised bed to build is the one which looks rather formal, but is well suited to edging a patio. This is made from paving stones or precast paving slabs which can often be purchased very cheaply in a slightly chipped condition. These are sunk in the ground edgewise at least 30cm deep. If they are hard up against the edge of the path or patio they will need no further support, otherwise they will need horizontally-laid slabs butted up hard against them. They are locked in position by 10cm of hardcore packed down tight inside before the soil is added. It is best to plant small trees and shrubs, as large specimens can easily damage the structure and will be very difficult to dig out once they have outgrown their home.

HEATHER GARDENS

Heather and some other lime-hating plants are well worth cultivating. They are tough and long-lived if you can create the right conditions, and they will need little maintenance. Nearly all species need neutral or acid soil. For most gardens this means creating a special area for them, and the easiest way to do this is to build a variation of raised beds using peat blocks. These hard blocks of compressed peat can be stacked into walls or terraces. They can be stood on concrete or laid directly on the soil, although in this case, hard water will slowly seep upwards and neutralize their acidity. Fill the planting area with a mixture of one part lime-free loam, one part peat and one part sand, and soak the whole thing thoroughly before planting the heathers.

On neutral or acid soils, plant directly into the ground, but add plenty of peat and some bone-meal. The treated soil should ideally be slightly springy, and not too damp and shaded. Heathers should be planted rather deep and firmed in well. If you provide the right conditions they spread very rapidly, and you can speed up this process by pegging healthy shoots on the outside of the plant flat against the soil, securing them in position with stones or wire. They will take a year to root adequately and can then be separated and transferred. Feed the plants annually with bone-meal and avoid the use of rich manure. Peat-block beds

unfortunately are not permanent and crumble slowly, so they will need occasional rebuilding.

Heathers come in a variety of sizes, some being moss-like in habit, while others form large shrubs. They need little maintenance other than clipping off old flower stems to encourage continuous flowering in the summer. Other suitable plants to grow in the heather bed are small rhododendrons ('azalea' type), gentians (gentiana), ferns and small lilies.

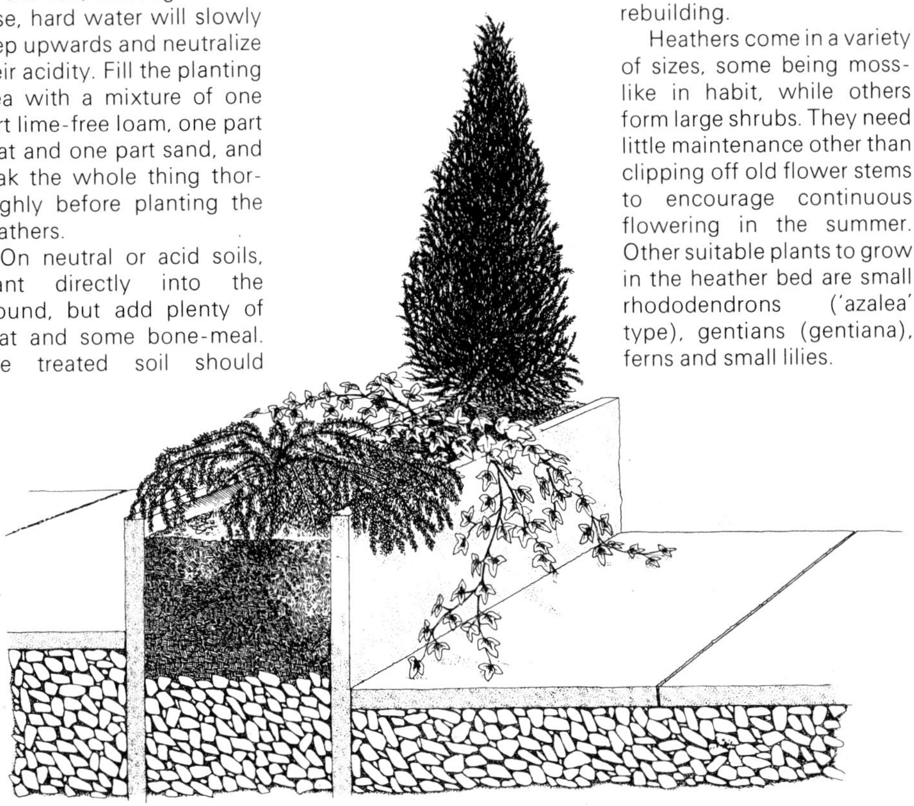

HEDGES

Most shrubs or trees can be used for hedging. However, few will tolerate the degree of pruning or trimming necessary to produce a neat urban hedge. If you are lucky enough to live in an area where you have space to experiment, try other types of hedging plant, such as cotoneaster, fuchsia, hydrangea, rosa, rhododendron or spiraea. A mixture of different types of shrub will give a more interesting informal hedge. For really quick and tough hedges, use the hawthorn (crataegus). This is fast-growing, but messy, and inclined to harbour many insect pests. It is useful on new estates to provide a rapid screen and can be dug out later when better plants have grown sufficiently.

Escallonia

If you are lucky enough to live near the sea and have a mild climate, escallonia makes a beautiful hedge. It is an evergreen with attractive red flowers, which will not, unfortunately, tolerate heavy frosts, although salt spray will not bother it.

Pyracantha   Beech

Box

A slow-growing, dwarf, evergreen hedge grown from box (buxus) has been used for centuries in formal gardens to edge flower beds and paths. It is very hardy provided it is kept moist in dry weather.

Cypress

The leyland cypress, X *Cupressocyparis leylandii* is a very rapid-growing evergreen, widely used for hedging. It will form a tall yet narrow hedge, ideal for the restricted space in a modern garden. Prune rather than clip to keep the attractive foliage healthy. It can reach a height of three metres within six years. Other conifers are equally satisfactory, but slower growing.

Privet

The choice of the Victorians for hedging, privet (ligustrum) will tolerate the foulest town air. It is fast-growing and hardy, but will kill most plants growing near it. The golden-leaved form is more attractive and less rampant. Clip back hard to avoid spindly growth and keep the hedge well tapered towards the top.

Beech

The ordinary or copper forms of beech (fagus) make an excellent but slow-growing hedge. It is deciduous, yet has the unusual benefit of retaining the dead leaves through the winter, adding colour and maintaining priv-

Escallonia   Privet   Chinese honeysuckle

acy. Beech is slow-growing, and needs cutting only once each year. It can be kept very narrow and will tolerate most soils and deep shade.

Holly

Holly (ilex) produces one of the best hedges. Only female plants bear berries, but male plants are also essential for pollination. Consequently try to obtain stock with the sexes identified or labelled so they can be alternated, avoiding large patches without berries. Prune rather than cut with shears, as damaged leaves are unsightly and persistent. It will thrive in sun or shade.

Yew

The yew (taxus) makes a dense evergreen hedge, which can be kept very narrow. Its usefulness is limited by several factors. The berries are very poisonous; the foliage is dark and prone to get dusty in towns; and the plant is extremely slow-growing. In spite of these drawbacks, yew makes a beautiful hedge if properly cared for.

Lonicera

Chinese honeysuckle, *Lonicera nitida*, makes a low, dense hedge, with small, neat leaves and tiny flowers. Little effort is needed to keep it tidy by clipping, but is not very robust and is easily damaged by children's games or by heavy snow.

Pyracantha

If you need a hedge in a dry exposed area, where there is plenty of sun, pyracantha is an ideal choice. It grows quite fast, and needs only light pruning rather than clipping. Varieties are available with red, orange or yellow berries. Too much clipping prevents berry formation.

Berberis

Berberis thunbergii atropurpurea (illustrated) makes a pretty purple-leaved hedge and is ideal for a town garden. Plant in sunny areas only and prune in the autumn to stop it becoming straggly. *Berberis stenophylla* makes a very pretty hedge. It has golden coloured foliage in spring, and yellow flowers and purple berries in the autumn. It is rather spiky, making a large, sprawling hedge, which may take up rather too much of a small garden.

Lavender

For sunny areas, lavender (lavandula) makes a fragrant, silvery hedge. It has a loose-growing habit, up to about half a metre in height. Cut back hard each year after flowering.

SHADY AREAS

Heavily-shaded areas pose a particular problem. Often the soil is unsuitable for all but the most vigorous plants. Where it is in the continual shade of a tree or buildings it becomes progressively less fertile, lacking the beneficial effect of continuous plant growth on soil structure. You can try and break this vicious cycle by planting trees or shrubs tolerant of shade and poor soil conditions. Alternatively you can make an attempt to improve matters by adding top soil and making sure light reaches the area. Preferably, do all these things.

There are some valuable plants which thrive, or at least survive, in heavily-shaded conditions. Not surprisingly, these trees and shrubs generally grow in woodland, where there is usually a lack of light. Betula

(birch), rhododendrons, arbutus and small species of salix (willow) will tolerate shade, while ivy will climb or creep enthusiastically in any light conditions. If your soil is suitable, camellias will thrive in a shaded and protected corner. Other flowering trees and shrubs are more difficult. The climbing hydrangea *Hydrangea petiolaris* will produce masses of white flowers in total shade, as will *Ligustrum ovalifolium*, related to privet. Conifers will grow in shade, but the green types can look very gloomy in these conditions, while the variegated and golden forms need more light.

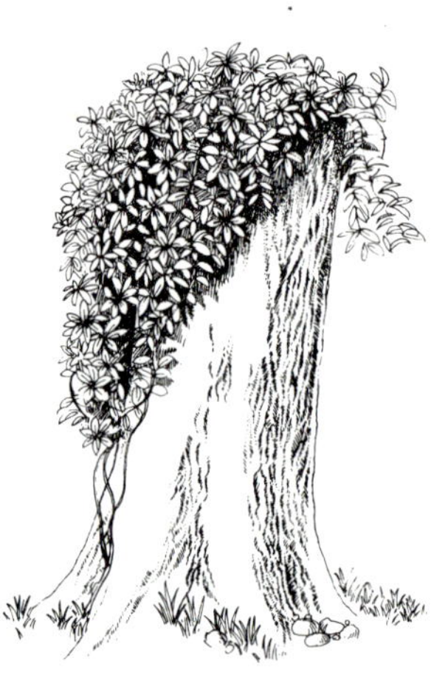

As herbaceous plants do not generally tolerate shade, it is worthwhile using creeping or prostrate trees and shrubs to provide ground cover. This holds in soil moisture and suppresses weed growth. The 30-cm Rose of Sharon (*Hypericum calycinum*) produces dense evergreen ground cover with masses of delicate yellow flowers throughout the summer. This plant and some creeping honeysuckles (lonicera) and ivies spread rapidly. Keep them under control, as once they reach

sunny areas, they will grow even faster. Bamboos of various species will also grow well in shade, but need restricting within a paved area if they are not to run riot through the garden.

CONTAINERS

Most trees and shrubs can be grown satisfactorily in containers. The advantages are that they can be moved about when necessary and that the restriction of roots checks growth and keeps the plant well under control. Against this you must consider whether containers will blend in with your garden

plan. You will also have to make arrangements for watering the plants if you holiday in the summer.

Suitable containers are easily acquired. Barrels and wooden tubs, stone troughs and old sinks, very large clay pots, or purpose-made concrete containers are all usable. But they must have a hole at the bottom for drainage. Without this, the tree or shrub will become waterlogged and the roots will rot. Place 5cm of coarse ballast or broken brick at the bottom of the container and fill with a mixture of 2 parts loam, 1 part peat, 1 part sand, plus a good helping of bone-meal. Pot-up exactly as you would a small plant, pressing down the compost very thoroughly. Do not forget a stake if the plant is tall, or will grow very tall.

Adequate feeding and watering is essential, as the plant will soon exhaust the limited supplies in the pot. When you go on holiday, stand the container on the soil in a damp corner, or better still, dig it in and pile the soil up around the pot.

If you have a greenhouse, delicate container-grown trees and shrubs such as fuchsias and bay trees can be moved into shelter during the winter. Otherwise, treat container plants in exactly the same way as those planted in the open ground, except for more careful and rigorous shaping and pruning.

WOODLAND

Few people are lucky enough to have a woodland garden. Most only have the opportunity when they take over a house with a thoroughly neglected garden and are confronted with a thicket full of rubbish to be cleared. But do not be too hasty to remove trees in such a thicket — just clear away the underbrush. The idea is to clear sufficient of the trees to provide a semi-shaded area. This will keep frost and cold winds away from delicate shrubs and trees. It also provides a moist habitat for shade-loving herbaceous plants such as ferns. The ideal condition to aim for is the dappled shade found naturally under birches (betula), and this means removing or thinning coarse-leaved trees such as sycamore (*Acer pseudaplatanus*) and plane (*Platanus* x *hispanica*) which produce very heavy shade.

All the plants previously listed for growing in shady areas are suitable for a woodland corner. Camellias and rhododendrons are especially suited to these conditions, where sun and wind cannot scorch their delicate blossom.

To get the best from your woodland garden, combine planting with winding paths, and construct banks to break up the ground contour. Do not ignore the possibility of changing the nature of your patch of woodland, or even creating your own, using rapidly-growing trees such as betula or *Chamaecyparis lawsoniana* which will grow rapidly even in among less attractive trees. As new trees develop, the older and less desirable trees can be progressively thinned or removed.

SHRUBBERY

To most modern gardeners, the old-fashioned shrubbery is an eyesore to be avoided at all costs. Fifty years or more ago, the shrubbery was a dense, drab green patch, containing large numbers of gloomy shrubs such as green privet (ligustrum), and Japanese laurel (aucuba). In the compact modern garden, there is no room for such uninteresting 'space-fillers'.

However, the shrubbery very definitely has a place. It is an area where you can demonstrate your knowledge and understanding of trees and shrubs. Use a shrubbery to provide contrast and colour with flowering and foliage plants. Conifers are ideal here. You can mix erect forms, weeping types and prostrate trees, in blues, greens, and brilliant yellows, and with a wide variety of foliage types. But never, ever, plant anything in your shrubbery unless you know exactly what it is, how fast, and how big it will grow. Otherwise, you risk damaging other valuable plants trying to remove a monster which has outgrown its proper site.

► Rose gardens like maximum sunlight. Shade and damp areas will encourage mildew and other diseases.

Propa-gation

Propagating shrubs and trees is a simple task—the easiest tend to propagate themselves. But most self-sown seedlings are not always as attractive as the parents. For this reason, and because seedlings are slower to get started, shrubs and trees are usually propagated vegetatively.

Layering

Layering is one of the simplest methods of producing new plants. Many even layer themselves without artificial aid, such as rhododendrons, magnolias and kalmias. All that is needed is to cut a small nick in the underside of one of the outer shoots and bend it on to the soil. It can be secured to the ground with a hair-pin-shaped piece of wire, or even with a stone. Cover the area in contact with the ground with a mixture of soil and peat and wait, probably for a year. The tip will grow vertically upwards, while roots spring from the buried section of branch. Once it is well rooted, and during the dormant period in the winter, the rooted layer can be severed and planted separately.

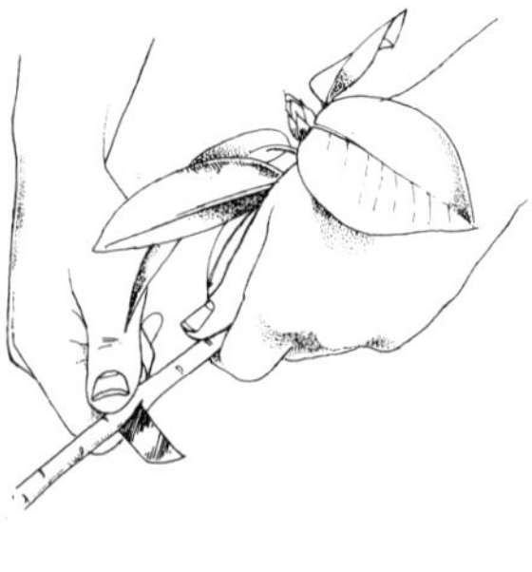

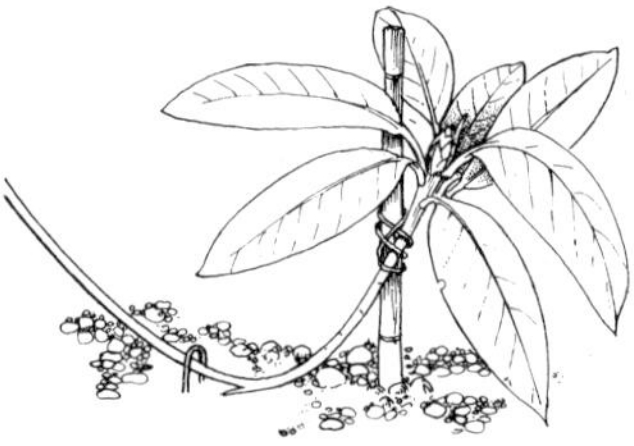

Air layering

If you cannot bend the branch down close enough to the soil, try the technique of air layering. To do this, first make a V-shaped nick in the bark of a shoot of the current year's growth, before the wood has become too hard. Wrap black polythene round the stem, securing it below the cut area with a rubber band. Fill the polythene cup you have created with a mixture of 1 part peat and 1 part loam or with a proprietary soil-less compost, and damp well. Now secure the rest of the polythene above the cut, using an elastic band, so the

compost is held firmly against the cut area. Roots will develop and spread into the compost. When they are large enough, cut away the shoot below the root ball, and remove the polythene before planting the rooted layer. This technique works best with fleshy-stemmed plants.

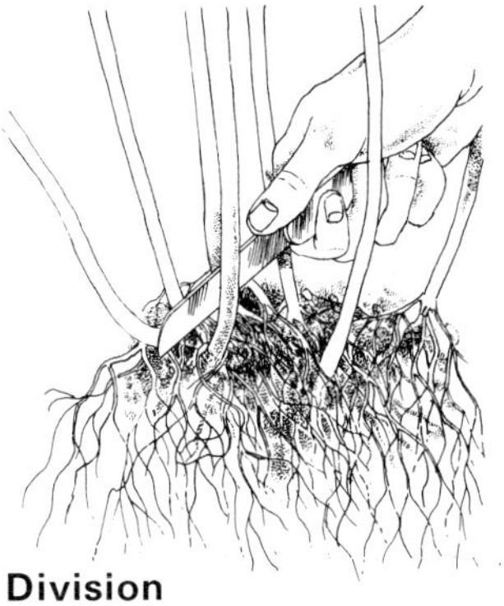

Division

Some small shrubs resemble herbaceous plants in their habit, forming dense clumps. Typical examples are vinca, small spiraeas, daboecia, some gaultherias, and kerria. Just as with the herbaceous clumps, these can be separated into a number of new plants. This means digging up the whole plant in early winter. Sections can be detached with a knife, particularly if suckers have developed. If the clump is very compact, force it apart by using two garden forks, held back-to-back, as levers. These plants usually grow very rapidly and each section will soon form another well-shaped shrub.

Cuttings

Cuttings require more care than the methods of propagating outlined above. The small shoot which is re-

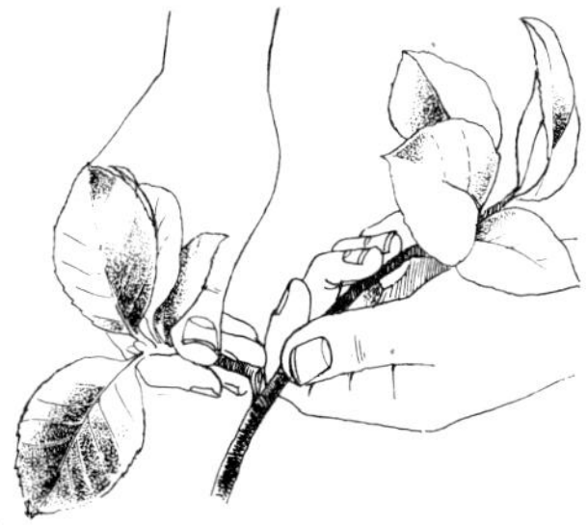

moved is very delicate and needs special attention to prevent it drying out before roots have formed. However, it does allow one to increase the stock of choice plants at no cost, as few people will object to you removing a small cutting from their tree or shrub.

Hardwood cuttings are the easiest to take. They are taken from the host plant in late autumn and are made by cutting just above a bud at the tip and just below a bud at the base. The whole cutting should be around 25cm in length. The cutting should 'strike' or root quite easily in any soil, but a mixture of peat and sand can be dug in and well-raked to encourage growth. Try to take hardwood cuttings at about the time their leaves fall and plant them with two-thirds of their length below the ground (make sure they are planted the right way up!). It will probably take at least a year before adequate roots develop.

Softwood cuttings are taken during the growing season and should not include the older, woody parts of the stems. The cutting will usually be 8 to 12cm long and should be from a healthy side-shoot. Some people like to make 'heel cuttings' including a small piece of the woody main stem, but this is not strictly necessary. Strip off the leaves from the length of the cutting and dip the stripped end in rooting hormone powder before planting to a

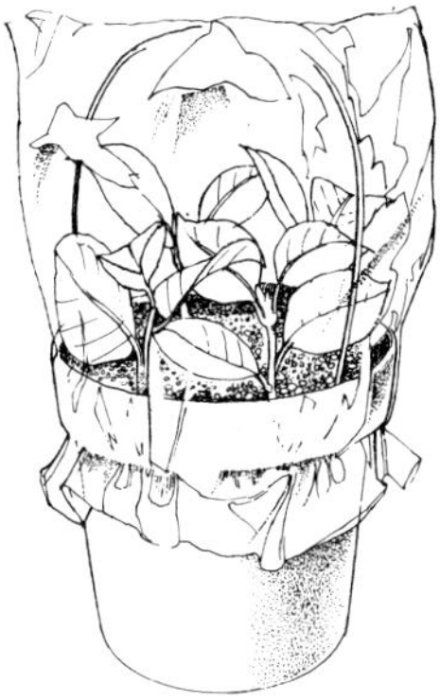

depth of 3 to 4cm in a mixture of peat and silver sand. Water loss can be damaging, so if your cuttings are small and tender, such as those of fuchsias, plant them in a pot and place the whole thing in a polythene bag, with wire to support the bag away from the cuttings, as shown in this illustration. But twigs can also be used. Otherwise, buy a propagator which will do the same job.

Large and robust softwood cuttings, such as those of buddleia, can be planted directly in the soil like hardwood cuttings. However, to minimize water loss cover well with a plastic cloche.

Cold frames, greenhouses and cloches

If you wish to grow cuttings on a larger scale, it is worth making or buying a cold frame, which will take large numbers of pot-grown cuttings. Tender cuttings can be easily protected from frost in such a way by covering loosely with straw

▶ The cloche is another useful aid for propagating cuttings or growing plants from seed. Its principal benefit is that it can be placed on a bed and removed later without disturbing the growing plants.

and sealing around the edges of the lid to prevent draughts.

For most growers of shrubs and trees the greenhouse is a luxury. However, it does allow more tender and exotic plants to be grown and prevents winter die-back in container-grown plants, such as hydrangeas and fuchsias. If grown outdoors all the year round, the plants expend much of their growth each spring in replacing the scorched foliage. If protected over winter, they can start the new year with healthy shoots and buds and so should thrive. Like the cold frame, the greenhouse is an ideal means of propagation, but care should be taken to harden-off plants raised this way. The young plants will become accustomed to the relatively high temperatures reached in even an unheated greenhouse and their growth will be fleshy and delicate. The shock of sudden exposure to the cold could kill them, so drop the temperature gradually by leaving vents or doors open for progressively longer periods.

Very inexpensive cloches can be obtained, made from polythene on a wire frame. They have to be pegged down very securely to protect them from winter gales. It is also a good idea to bury the edges of the polythene in the soil to stop draughts getting inside. Other types can be bought ready-made or can be assembled from sheets of glass, with metal clips holding the edges together.

Growing from seed

Trees and shrubs are not always easy to grow from seed, but if you wish to try, the cloche is an ideal aid. Germination of the seed can take over a year, as with some tough seeds there is a complicated interplay between temperature, the seasons and possibly bacterial action on the seed coat before growth can begin. The seedlings are usually delicate and dislike being transplanted, so it is best to

sow directly into a prepared bed and cover with a cloche, which can be removed as the young plants develop. Allow plenty of ventilation beneath cloches in warm weather as the temperature can rise very rapidly.

▶ A greenhouse can be used as a convenient store for useful garden accessories as well as a place for propagating and growing delicate shrubs and trees.

Plants for the greenhouse

The greenhouse can be used to grow perfect displays of plants such as Japanese azaleas (rhododendron), camellias, fuchsias or hydrangeas. These plants can be grown in containers, allowing growth to start safely in the early spring without fear of frost damage. On the point of flowering, the containers can be moved out to a patio.

Fuchsias, for example, need a warm, moist atmosphere, especially for early growth. Outdoors all the year round they are severely cut back by frost. In the greenhouse, by careful pinching-out, it is easy to encourage them to form standards or pyramids, and they can be moved outdoors when the weather is suitable.

Tub-grown fuchsias and hydrangeas should be brought back into the greenhouse before the start of the really hard weather. Even the unheated greenhouse provides adequate protection against frost, provided there are no draughts. Tub-grown shrubs are particularly susceptible to frost if grown without protection, as the relatively small amount of soil in the container cools off far more rapidly than does the ground.

Pests and diseases

Trees and shrubs are generally robust and can shrug off diseases and pests which would kill more tender herbaceous plants. However, their appearance can be ruined by a large number of factors and it pays to take the trouble of recognizing these problems so that the appropriate measures can be taken.

INSECT PESTS

Aphids

The greenfly or aphid attacks most shrubs and trees, but does not often cause obvious damage. The parasites suck sap from the most delicate new growth which is often distorted as a result. In addition, the aphid carries many virus diseases of trees and shrubs, particularly those causing leaf curl and discoloration. Destroy aphids by regular spraying as soon as the first signs appear. Spray shoots particularly thoroughly and on the undersides of leaves, where the insects congregate. Use a grease band on the trunk of heavily affected trees to keep ants away. Ants actually 'farm' aphids, carrying them to trees formerly free of infestation.

Woolly aphids

The cotton-wool-like patches caused by woolly aphids are very unsightly. They respond best to regular spraying with pesticides containing malathion or Gamma-BHC. Spray with tar oil in the winter to destroy dormant aphids and their eggs.

Capsid bugs

These insects look rather like large aphids and similarly feed on the plant sap. Control in the same way.

Caterpillars

Caterpillars are not often a serious nuisance in trees and shrubs, but occasionally they become very common locally and cause much damage because of their big appetites. Due to their relatively large size they need heavy applications of insecticides to get rid of them and special application rates are recommended on the packs. Derris, Gamma-BHC and malathion are all effective.

Leaf-cutter bees

These pests resemble the domestic hive bee. They chop out pieces from the leaves of roses, rhododendron, labernum and syringa using them to line their nests.

Leaf miners

Shrubs and trees are often attacked by these insect larvae, which make unsightly tracks on the leaf surface. But applications of malathion provide effective control. Leaf miners commonly affect holly.

Spider mites

These tiny parasites cause damage to foliage, which turns brown and falls prematurely. They are especially common in very hot weather. Control with winter washes, most insecticides or with lime sulphur.

Sawfly

This pest is particularly common on roses, folding the leaf over to protect the eggs and the young. Spray regularly with malathion as soon as signs appear.

Scale insects

These sucking insects look like blisters on the bark or leaves. Their bites introduce a number of diseases and cause distortion of the tender new growth. Their waxy surface makes them resistant to many insecticides and a winter wash with tar oil is probably the most satisfactory method of control.

DISEASES

Peach-leaf curl

This fungal disease attacks many decorative fruit trees, starting as red blisters, then spreading to destroy large parts of plant. It is controlled by sprays with Bordeaux mixture or other fungicides. Cut off and burn all infected stems.

Honey fungus

This is the most damaging of all parasites to shrubs and trees. It produces long black threads which spread into the roots and under the bark. Its first signs are gold-coloured toadstools springing up round the base of the tree, which by then is doomed. Dig it up and burn completely, and do not replant in the area for at least a year.

Black spot

This is a fungal disease peculiar to roses, with some varieties especially susceptible. The spots usually only appear towards the end of the flowering season. Control by repeated spraying with a systemic fungicide.

Rust disease

This attacks roses in warmer areas only. It produces bright orange speckles all over the plant and is difficult to treat. Destroy badly affected bushes or spray with copper-based fungicides.

Silver leaf

This is a serious disease of many ornamental shrubs and trees. Affected leaves have a silvery glint to them and when cut the stems are stained dark inside. The treatment is to cut back into healthy wood, removing and burning all the affected material.

Mildew

This is a powdery deposit on leaves and buds, which gradually spreads and causes leaf drop. Spray regularly with a proprietary fungicide from as soon as the first signs appear.

Coral spot

This appears as tiny pink specks on dying wood. Treat by cutting out all the dead wood as soon as it is noticed, cutting back well into the living wood.

PHYSICAL PROBLEMS

Scorching and wilting almost always follow planting-out of a new tree or shrub in an exposed area. It is caused by a rapid evaporation of water from the leaves, which is too fast to allow replacement by the poorly established roots. Protect the plant with plastic sheeting for a few months until the roots are developed. Possibly the plant is too delicate for its situation and could be replaced with a hardier substitute.

High winds at the time when the buds are opening can also cause scorching of the tips. Dainty leaves like those of the acer are very prone to this damage. There is only one solution, which is to keep the wind off. Either transplant to a more sheltered spot or screen the plant each spring until the new leaves have become established.

Chlorosis

Yellowing of the leaves is very common in large-leaved evergreens such as rhododendron and camellia. It is caused by either too much lime in the soil or by too little iron; the presence of large amounts of lime prevents the plant from taking in the iron it needs to make chlorophyll. Apply a compound called iron sequestrene, which is very expensive, but can have dramatic effects on the health of acid-loving plants. The application will need to be repeated each year, so perhaps it is cheaper in the long run to replace affected plants with something more suited to your local soil conditions.

A–Z of shrubs and trees

Abbreviations

T = Tree
S = Shrub
C = Conifer
Cl = Climber
D = Deciduous
E = Evergreen
Se = Semi-evergreen
Syn. = Synonym

The trees, shrubs and climbers listed here are but a very few of the many available to use for year round decoration of a garden. As many different types of hardy plants as possible have been selected to serve a variety of purposes: single specimen trees; wind-break, hedge, border, rockery or ground cover shrubs; and decorative climbers to cover structures and hide eyesores. The catalogues of nurserymen and good garden centres should also be consulted when making a selection of these plants as new and often better varieties are introduced from time to time.

Average heights and spreads of plants are given, but these can vary according to growing conditions.

Abelia S,D

Shrubs which are free-flowering in summer and autumn and grow well in most soils but prefer a sheltered sunny position. Leaves are usually ovate, and sometimes semi-evergreen. Flowers, summer and early autumn, are tubular and pale pink. Those most usually grown are *Abelia* x *grandiflora* (**1**), height and spread up to 2·7m, and *A. schumanii,* height and spread about 3m. Propagate by 7·5- to 10-cm cuttings of current season's shoots in summer. Prune old wood after flowering.

Abies C,T,E

Fir

Trees which are usually conical in shape and have needle-like leaves of various shades of green. Will grow in most soils. Cones are produced, often a bluish colour when young. There are a number of species, from large trees suitable as specimens to small slow-growing ones for a rockery. *Abies koreana*, about 5m high, and *A. lasiocarpa*, up to 3m with silver blue leaves, make attractive garden trees, and the dwarf slow growing forms of *A. balsamea* (**2**), height and spread about 1m, are useful in shrubbery or rockery. Propagation is difficult so it is advisable to buy plants. Pruning is unnecessary, except if too strong side shoot or shoots appear to unbalance symmetry of trees, in which case remove flush with trunk in spring.

Acer T,S,D

Maple, Japanese Maple

Trees and shrubs of varying heights, grown more for the colour of their leaves in summer and autumn than for their flowers, though their key-shaped seeds are attractive. Will grow in most soils but prefer protection from early morning sun. The leaves are palmate, usually five-lobed, and vary in colour from pale green, green and white, pink and purple in spring and summer to many shades of yellow and red in autumn. Sometimes the trunk bark shows snake-like markings or peels in autumn to give varying colours. Useful trees for the garden are *Acer capillipes, A. negundo, A. platinoides* (**3**) and varieties, *A. griseum* and *A. rufinerve,* growing between 4 and 10m plus. The Japanese Maples, varieties of *Acer japonicum* and *A. palmatum,* are between 60cm and 5m or more in height and spread. Propagation is by seeds sown in autumn or by grafting in spring of coloured forms. Pruning is unnecessary.

Actinidia Cl,D

Only two of these unusual but easily grown twining plants are generally available. They like a well-drained rich soil and a wall, tree or some form of support up which to grow. Initially, tie in young growths to supports. *Actinidia chinensis* will grow up to 8 to 9m, has dark green, heart-shaped leaves, creamy flowers in summer, sometimes followed by hairy edible fruits (Chinese gooseberries). *A. kolomikta* (**4**) grows 2 to 4m, has green heart-shaped leaves with white and pink tips, and white flowers in early summer. Propagate from seeds or summer cuttings in heat. Prune out unwanted growths in late winter.

Amelanchier T/S,D

Snowy Mespilus, June Berry

Amelanchier canadensis (**5**, syn. *A. laevis*) is the only species in common cultivation and forms a large shrub unless trained as a tree. Height and spread 4 to 8m. Plant in any good soil. It bears long sprays of white flowers in spring, crimson fruits in early summer and the woolly, ovate and toothed leaves open pinkish-green and turn red or yellow in autumn. Propagate by seeds sown in a cold frame in summer, layering branches in autumn, or removing rooted suckers in winter. Pruning is unnecessary.

Arbutus T,S,E
Strawberry Tree
Very ornamental trees or large shrubs, 3 to 6m high, with dark green, shiny leaves and often attractively coloured stems and bark. Plant in well-drained good soil, preferably lime-free though the two species commonly grown, *Arbutus andrachnoides* (syn. *A.* x *hybrida*) and *A. unedo* (**6**), are lime-tolerant. White flowers and 'strawberry' fruits are carried together in late autumn and early winter on the latter, but in spring on the former, which is usually grown for its red bark rather than its fruits. Propagation by seeds or summer heel cuttings is slow and it is advisable to buy plants. Prune straggly shoots in spring and remove lower growths from tree trunks to show bark.

Aucuba S,E
Spotted Laurel
Bushy round shrub, about 2m in height and spread, with shiny dark green ovate leaves, often spotted or striped. Unisexual so necessary to plant both sexes to produce berries on female plants from autumn to spring. Flowers, olive green, in panicles, are borne in spring. Easily grown in any soil, in sun or shade, and in containers. *Aucuba japonica* (**7**) and its many varieties are widely grown. Propagation is by heel cuttings in late summer. Prune old shoots to 60 to 90cm long in spring.

Azalea
see **Rhododendron,** page 80

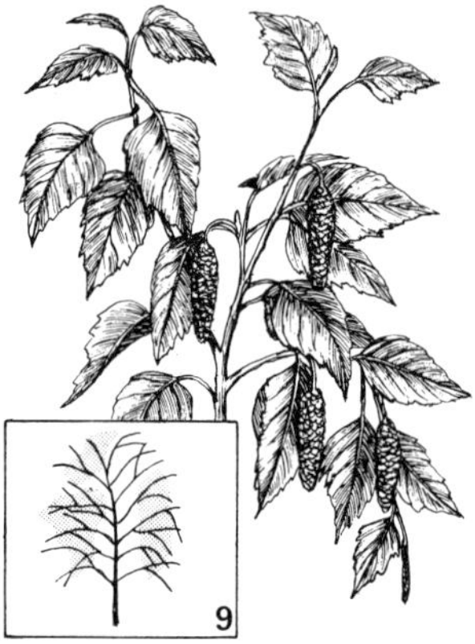

Berberis S,D,E
Barberry
A large genus of many evergreen and deciduous shrubs which are easy to grow in any well drained soil and in sunny or shady positions. All are spiny and most have small lanceolate leaves, and clusters of tubular yellow or orange flowers in late spring. Some species, hybrids and varieties are suitable for hedges, set 60cm apart. The deciduous barberries are grown mainly for their long lasting ornamental berries and brilliantly coloured leaves in autumn and winter. Useful plants in this group are: *Berberis* x *rubrostilla*, red fruits, grey-green leaves, height about 1·2m, spread about 2m; *B. thunbergii* and its varieties, with red fruits, and the plants varying in size from 1·2m high by 2m wide to dwarf compact forms for the rockery; and *B. wilsonae*, coral red berries, arching branches, and a height and spread of about 1m.
Among the evergreens are: *Berberis darwinii* (**8**), deep orange flowers, blue berries and holly-like leaves growing up to 2·5m high and spreading about 2m; *B. gagnepainii*, black berries, reddish stems, about 1·5m by 1·2m; *B. linearifolia* and its well-known form 'Orange King', with deep orange to red flowers, purple berries with a waxy bloom, height up to 3m, spread about 1m; *B* x *stenophylla* with arching sprays of yellow flowers but few fruits, about 3m by 3m, and its compact dwarf forms about 30cm high; and *B. verruculosa*, with glossy green leaves, white underneath, drooping yellow flowers followed by black fruits (leaves also tend to colour in autumn), about 1·5m by 1·5m. Propagate by sowing seeds in the open in early winter, or heel cuttings of lateral shoots in late summer. Prune by trimming to shape after flowering or in winter after fruiting; if severe pruning is necessary do so in winter with deciduous species and after flowering with evergreens.

Betula T,D
Birch
Mostly grown for their attractive bark which generally becomes silvery and peels with age. Their graceful habit and usually ovate leaves, which turn yellow in autumn, make these fine specimen trees. Yellowish-green male and female catkins are borne in spring. Will grow well in any soil but rooting is shallow so do not underplant. *Betula ermanii* and *B. pendula* (**9**) and its weeping shaped forms are most commonly grown. Their height is 4 to 8m and spread 2 to 4m. Propagation is by seed in spring in a cold frame. Pruning is unnecessary.

Buddleia T,S,D,E,Se
Butterfly Bush
Small trees and shrubs which grow well in any soil but prefer plenty of sun to perform to best advantage. The flowers are usually borne summer and autumn in plume-like sprays, sometimes globular-shaped; most are fragrant and the colours are shades of purple, blue, pink, white or orange. The leaves are ovate or lanceolate and in some species more or less evergreen. All grow up to about 2·5m high with a spread of about 2m. Good species to select are *Buddleia alternifolia*, best as a tree to show its weeping habit, *B. davidii* (**10**) and its varieties in a wide colour range and often with silvery-grey leaves, and *B. globosa*, with its bushy habit and clusters of orange flower

11

12

13

balls. Propagation is by heel cuttings in summer. Prune *B. davidii* and its varieties hard back in spring to within 5 to 7·5cm, and the others as necessary after flowering to keep the shape of the tree or bush.

Buxus S,E
Box
Only one species, *Buxus sempervirens* (**11**), and its many varieties are commonly grown, either as evergreen hedging of different heights (with plants set 30cm apart), or as specimens, often for topiary. Grows easily in any soil or situation. Its evergreen glossy leaves are usually oblong, and the spring flowers are pale green and insignificant. Ultimate height and spread can be about 3m by 2m, but by hard clipping in late summer the bushes or hedges can be kept to the required size and shape. Propagation is by late summer cuttings 7·5 to 10cm long grown on for two years.

Calluna S,E
Heather, Ling
Although only one species, *Calluna vulgaris* (**12**), it has very many varieties. All grow well in a lime-free soil and prefer a sunny position. They can be used as specimen plants, in a rockery or for ground cover, and their height and spread varies from about 7·5 to 75cm. The leaves are small and lance-shaped and often golden, grey, bronze or red as well as green. The flowering period, depending on variety, is from summer to early winter, the bell-shaped blooms, carried on spikes, varying in colour from purple, pink or white. Propagation is by cuttings 2·5 to 5cm long taken in late summer and rooted in a mist propagator, or by layering in early spring. Prune in early spring by removing the old flowering spikes, which are often attractive during the winter. (see also **Daboecia** page 65 and **Erica** page 66.)

Camellia T,S,E
A genus of mainly hardy, evergreen shrubs and some trees which grow well in an acid peaty soil with leaf mould or shredded bark, both dug into the soil and used as a mulch. They like a semi-shady position where early morning spring sun will not damage the blooms, so grow them in a north or west facing site, or among trees. Some varieties do well grown in containers of an acid compost. The leaves are ovate and glossy green and the large flowers, up to 15cm across, of pink, red, white or bicoloured, with yellow stamens borne in winter or spring, are cup-shaped and single, semi-double, double or anemone-shaped (one or two rows of large petals with a centre of small petals). The varieties of *Camellia japonica* and *C.* x *williamsii* (**13**) are as hardy as laurels, are most commonly grown, and there is a large selection from which to choose. The *C. japonica* forms can grow up to 4m with a spread of about 3m; the *C. williamsii* group are slightly smaller. Propagation is by 7·5 to 10cm long cuttings in summer with bottom heat, or by layering in early autumn. Little pruning is required, except to remove unwanted or straggly shoots in spring, especially if the plants are grown against a wall and the shoots tied in to supports. Dead head all *C. japonica* forms after flowering.

Catalpa T,D
Indian Bean Tree
Catalpa bignonioides (**14**), and its yellow leaved form 'Aurea',

are good town trees, growing up to 10m and forming round heads. They like a rich soil and sunny position. The heart-shaped leaves are aromatic when crushed and are not fully formed until early summer. Foxglove-like flowers of white spotted yellow and purple are carried in erect sprays in summer; they are followed by bean-like seed pods. Propagation by summer heel cuttings in heat. Pruning is unnecessary.

Ceanothus T,S,E,D
Californian Lilac

Among the best of blue flowering shrubs, the deciduous types are completely hardy but the evergreen ones are best given the protection of a sheltered south facing wall. Plant in good soil which does not contain much chalk. The leaves are usually ovate, sometimes downy on the under surface. The flowers are borne in clusters, on the deciduous types from mid summer to mid autumn, and on the evergreen forms from spring to mid summer. Height and spread is usually up to 3m, and these can be used for tying against walls, but others are smaller and more branching, making them suitable as ground cover plants. Good evergreen types are *Ceanothus* x 'Autumnal Blue', *C.* x *burkwoodii*, *C. impressus* and *C. thyrsiflorus*, while of the deciduous forms, the varieties of *C. hybridus*, such as 'Gloire de Versailles' (**15**), are recommended. Propagation is by 7·5- to 10-cm heel cuttings in summer in heat. Little pruning of evergreen forms is required but cut back shoots of deciduous varieties to about 10cm from the old wood in spring.

Chaenomeles (syn. Cydonia) S,D
Japonica, Japanese Quince
Shrubs which grow well in most soils and when trained against sunny walls, though they are also effective as specimens in a shrub border. The leaves are rounded and glossy or downy green, and the cup-shaped flowers are borne in small clusters, usually red, orange, pink or white, from as early as mid-winter through to mid-summer. Apple-shaped, fragrant yellow fruits, which are edible, often follow in autumn. Varieties and forms of *Chaenomeles japonica*, *C. speciosa* (**16**, syn. *C. lagenaria*), and *C.* x *superba* are most commonly grown. Height and spread of them all is about 2m or less. Propagation is by 10-cm long summer heel cuttings in heat, layering shoots in early autumn (which can take two years) or seeds sown in a cold frame and grown on for three to five years. Prune specimen shrubs only to keep them in shape, and tie in and cut back to two to three buds shoots of wall-trained plants in early summer.

Chamaecyparis (syn. Cupressus) C,T,E
False Cypress
Slow and fast growing conifers which grow well in any position and can be used as specimens, screening trees, for hedging, ground cover or rockery planting. The needle leaves are flattened and carried in flat sprays and are green, bluish-grey or golden in colour. Sometimes small cones are produced. The trees can be conical or rounded in shape. The most commonly grown species are *Chamaecyparis lawsoniana* (**17**), *C. obtusa* and *C. pisifera* and their many varieties. The species reach 20m or more in height, but their varieties vary in height and spread from dwarf forms as small as 30cm by 60cm up to about 5m by 3m. Propagation is by seed sown under glass or heel cuttings about 10cm long in mid-winter or late spring. No pruning is required other than to remove forked branches and maintain the leading shoot. Hedging *C. lawsoniana* (plants set 60cm apart) can be clipped in late spring.

Chimonanthus S,D
Winter Sweet
Only one species, *Chimonanthus praecox* (**18**), and its varieties are grown for their pale yellow, sometimes red- or purple-centred, very fragrant cup-shaped flowers borne in winter. The scented lanceolate leaves appear later in spring. Grows well in any position, including chalky soils, but flowers best against a sunny wall. Height and spread about 3m. Propagate by seeds in heat in autumn, or layering in late summer. Prune lightly to retain shape after flowering.

Choisya S,E
Mexican Orange Blossom
A bushy evergreen shrub that grows up to 3m tall with a spread of about 2m. The dark green, shiny, trifoliate leaves are fragrant when crushed and the sweetly scented clusters of white star-like flowers are borne in late spring and intermittently until early winter. *Choisya ternata* (**19**) is the species usually grown. Propagation is by 7·5- to 10-cm cuttings in summer in heat. Prune lightly, removing straggly or dead shoots, after main flowering.

Cistus S,E
Rock Rose, Sun Rose
Evergreen shrubs, ideal for hot dry positions and chalky soil. The lanceolate leaves vary in colour from light to dark green or grey, and the five petalled white or pink flowers, often with a coloured central blotch and prominent yellow stamens, are produced daily in late spring and summer. The shrubs grow between 1 to 2m high and spread about 60 to 100cm. *Cistus* x *corbariensis*, *C.* x *cyprius*, *C. laurifolius*, *C.* x *purpureus* (**20**), *C.* 'Silver Pink', and *C.* x *skanbergii* are good species and hybrids to choose. Propagate by seeds in spring, or 10-cm long cuttings in summer, both in a cold frame. Prune lightly after flowering to remove straggly or dead shoots.

Clematis Cl, E,D,Se
Virgin's Bower
Popular for decorating walls, trellis, fences, old trees, arches, pergolas or anything which enables them to climb with the

support of their twining leaf stalks; they may need tying in when grown against a solid surface such as a wall. The leaves, deciduous or evergreen, are compound with three or more leaflets. The usually four-petalled saucer-, bell- or urn-shaped flowers, of purple, pink, mauve, red, yellow or white, are borne more or less at any time of year depending on which species or hybrids are grown. They grow anything up to 10m in height and spread. All like a good, deep, cool root-run, preferably with crushed chalk in the sub-soil, and should be mulched annually to keep the root area cool. They flower best if the climbing shoots get full sun.

The genus is divided broadly into two groups, the species and the hybrids, the latter with the largest flowers. The hybrids are prone to clematis wilt disease and should be sprayed in spring with a copper fungicide if necessary and diseased stems cut out and burned. Popular species are *Clematis armandii* (E), *C. flammula* (D), *C. florida* (Se), *C. macropetala* (D), *C. montana* (D) and *C. tangutica* (D), and there are good varieties produced from some. There are very many large flowered garden hybrids from which to choose, such as 'Comtesse de Bouchaud', 'Ernest Markham', 'Jackmanii', 'Nelly Moser' (**21**), 'Perle d'Azur', and 'The President'. Propagation is by 10-cm stem cuttings in summer in heat, seeds sown in autumn, or by layering in mid-spring. Pruning back all hybrid clematis to 15 to 25cm from ground level after planting is advisable. Thereafter prune late spring flowering varieties lightly after flowering, removing dead and straggly shoots; prune summer flowering varieties similarly in early spring; and cut back late summer and autumn flowering varieties to within 10 to 15cm of the previous year's growth in early spring. Very overgrown plants can be cut back to 60 to 75cm.

Cornus T,S,D
Dogwood, Cornel
Small trees and shrubs grown mainly for their coloured bark, attractive leaves and autumn berries. The leaves are usually ovate and green, or variegated with white or yellow. The flowers are small and usually white or yellow and borne in clusters, sometimes surrounded by pink or white bracts. The fruits are blue or red. In autumn the leaves colour well and fall to reveal yellow or red stems in some varieties. All do well in good soil and a sunny position, where they colour best, but will stand partial shade. Height and spread are about 2·5m by 1·75m for tree forms and approximately 1·75m by 1·5m for shrubs. Good species are *Cornus alba* and its varieties, and *C. stolonifera* for its leaf and bark colours, *C. florida* and *C. kousa* (**22**) for coloured bracts, and *C. mas* for red berries. Propagation is by cuttings 10cm long in summer in heat or rooted suckers. Prune the shrubby species hard back to about 20 to 25cm from the ground in spring, but only cut out dead or unshapely stems from tree species.

Corylopsis S,D
Corylopsis spicata (**23**) is popularly grown for its scented sprays of yellow bell-shaped flowers in early and mid-spring.

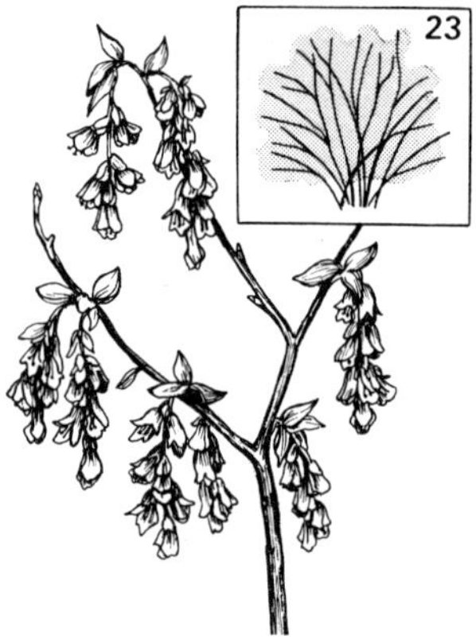

The heart-shaped green leaves follow. The plants like a good soil with peat dug in, and prefer a sheltered position against a sunny wall or in a border protected by other shrubs or trees. Height is about 2 to 3m and spread 1·5 to 2m. Propagation is by layering in late autumn. Pruning is usually unnecessary.

Cotinus (syn. Rhus) T,S,D
Smoke Tree
The two species most commonly grown, *Cotinus americanus* and *C. coggygria* (**24**) and its varieties (including the purple-leaved forms), are rounded in shape and have ovate leaves which colour brilliantly in autumn. The summer flowers are greenish-white or pink turning to smoke-grey and give a hazy appearance. Any soil in a sunny position is suitable. Height and spread is about 3m. Propagation is by autumn layering. Prune out straggly shoots in spring.

Cotoneaster T,S,E,D,Se
An ornamental genus of evergreen, semi-evergreen, and deciduous plants that grow in any soil and any position and provides subjects suitable for specimen trees, shrubberies, hedges, screening, rockeries and ground cover. Pink or white saucer-shaped flowers appear in profusion in early summer and are followed by long-lasting bright coloured berries in autumn. The ovate or lanceolate leaves often colour brilliantly in autumn. Among tree forms growing about 5m by 5m are *Cotoneaster* 'Cornubia' (**25**, Se), *C.* x *rothschildianus* (Se) and *C* x *watereri* (Se). *C. lacteus* (E), *C. franchetii* (E), and *C. simonsii* (Se), 3 by 2·5m, make good hedging plants set 30 to 90cm apart. Among the general shrubby species, *C. bullatus* (D), *C. wardii* (E), *C. conspicuus* (E) and *C. salicifolius* (E) grow about 2m high and spread about 1·5 to 2m. Low growing forms, with a height up to 60cm but a spread of 1·5m or more, include *C. horizontalis* (D), *C. microphyllus* (E), and *C.* 'Skogholm' (E). Propagation by seed sown in autumn in a cold frame, by 7·5 to 10cm long cuttings in late summer, or layering in late autumn. Prune only if necessary, cutting back to shape evergreen species in late spring and deciduous forms in late winter, or early autumn if hedging.

Crataegus T,S,D
Hawthorn, May, Ornamental Thorn
Hardy and tolerant thorny trees and shrubs for growing in any soil in an open position. Make good specimen lawn trees, and *Crataegus monogyna* is useful for hedging (set 30cm apart). White, pink or red clusters of single or double flowers are borne in late spring, and are followed in autumn by orange or red fruits. The leaves are ovate or lobed and often produce rich autumn colours. Good species include *Crataegus carrierei*, (syn. *C. lavallei*), *C. oxycantha* (**26**) and its varieties, and *C. prunifolia*. Height and spread are 5 to 6m. Propagation is difficult, so best to buy plants. Pruning is unnecessary except for hedge trimming in summer.

Cryptomeria C,T,E
Japanese Cedar
Only one species, *Cryptomeria*

24

25

26

japonica (**27**), which is a large, conical-shaped, fast-growing tree with awl-shaped leaves and rounded cones. *C. j* 'Elegans', ultimately 4 to 6m high by 3 to 4m wide, is the most commonly grown variety and is exceptional in that its green evergreen foliage turns red in autumn. A number of small bushy growing forms, 1m by 1m or less, are available also for rock gardens or small border specimens. All like a slightly acid, deep soil. Propagation is by 5- to 10-cm cuttings in early autumn in a cold frame. No pruning is required except to trim to shape.

X Cupressocyparis C,T,E
Leyland Cypress
This is a genus of one hybrid species, X *Cupressocyparis leylandii* (**28**) and its varieties. Its rapid growth and columnar habit make it ideal for hedges and screening. The scale-like triangular leaves are green,

greyish or yellow and sometimes small roundish cones are formed. Ultimate height can be 20m by 5m spread. Grows well in deep soils in sun or light shade. Stake firmly initially to maintain upright position. Set hedging plants 60 to 75cm apart. Propagation is by 10-cm lateral shoots in autumn outdoors. Prune hedges in early autumn and remove main shoots when desired height of hedge reached.

Cytisus S,D

Broom

Free flowering shrubs with fragrant sprays in early summer of yellow, white, red or bicoloured sweet-pea-shaped flowers and trifoliate leaves or almost leafless, green stems. They grow best in sandy soils and like full sun. *Cytisus scoparius* (**29**) and its many hybrids and varieties are most often grown and when mature are about 2·5m by 2·5m, or slightly less for *C. praecox*. For rock gardens, *C.* x *beanii*, *C.* x *kewensis*, *C. purgans* and *C. purpureus* are good spreading plants about 60cm high and 120cm wide. Taller growing species, up to 3m, include *C. albus* and *C. battandieri*. All dislike root disturbance so plant from pots. Propagation by seeds in late spring or 7·5- to 10–cm cuttings in late summer in a cold frame. Most require no pruning but if necessary cut back previous years shoots after flowering.

Daboecia S,E

Irish Bell Heather, St. Dabeoc's Heath

Daboecia cantabrica (**30**) and its varieties are most widely grown. They like an acid, peaty soil and are attractive in a heather garden, rockery or for ground cover. The small dark green leaves are silvery beneath and the purple, pink or white bell-shaped flowers are carried on long stems from late spring to winter. Height and spread are 30 to 60cm. Propagation and pruning as for **Calluna,** see page 59.

Daphne S,E,D,Se

Easily grown as front of border or rockery shrubs in good soil in sun or light shade. They produce tubular, pink, reddish or white fragrant flowers in clusters in winter to early summer according to species or varieties. These are sometimes followed by coloured berries. The leaves are ovate or lanceolate and the shrubs vary in size from a height of 15cm to 3m and a spread of 30cm to 3m. The earliest to flower are *Daphne mezereum* (D) and *D. odora* (E) and their varieties followed by *D.* x *burkwoodii* (Se), *D. cneorum* (**31**, E) and *D. collina* (E) and their various forms. Propagate by 5- to 10-cm long heel cuttings in late summer in a cold frame. No pruning is required except to remove straggly shoots in mid-spring.

Deutzia S,D

Hardy, easy to grow, reliable early summer flowering shrubs for town or country, they like a good soil, even if chalky, and a sunny position. The bark is brown and often peels, the leaves are ovate or lanceolate and the white, pink or purple flowers are borne in clusters along long stems in summer. Height is about 1·2 to 2m and spread 1 to 2m. Good species and their varieties to grow are *Deutzia* x *elegantissima* (**32**), *D.* x *hybrida*, *D.* x *kalmiflora*, *D.* x *rosea* and *D. scabra*. Propagation by 7·5- to 10-cm long lateral shoots in summer in a cold frame or 30-cm hardwood cuttings outdoors in autumn. Prune old flowering stems close to ground level in mid-summer to encourage fresh growth.

Elaeagnus S,E,Se

Mainly grown for the decorative foliage and orange-brown twigs and shoots. They make good hedging and screening plants set about 45cm apart. The leaves are ovate and green, variegated yellow, or have silvery undersurfaces. The flowers, if any, are inconspicuous, silvery white, and followed by autumn berries. All are hardy, drought resistant and grow in any soil and a sunny or lightly shaded position. Most commonly grown species and their varieties are *Elaeagnus* x *ebbingii* (E), *E. macrophylla* (E), *E. pungens* (**33**, E), and *E. umbellata* (Se). Height and spread are from 1·5 to 3m. Propagation is by 7·5- to 10-cm cuttings in late summer in a cold frame. Prune straggly shoots in late spring and remove green-leaved shoots from variegated-leaved varieties as they appear. Trim hedges in early summer and early autumn.

Enkianthus S,D

Useful shrubs for shady places, but must have an acid soil and annual top dressing of peat. Leaves ovate or elliptic, green in summer but brightly coloured red or orange in autumn. Flowers, usually bell-shaped, small, borne in clusters and yellow or white, often with red veins, appear in late spring. Commonly grown species are *Enkianthus campanulatus* (**34**), *E. cernuus* and *E. perulatus*. Height and spread about 2m by 1m. Propagate by heel cuttings 7·5 to 10cm long in late summer in a cold frame. Pruning is unnecessary except to remove dead or unwanted growths.

Erica S,E
Heather, Heath
Shrubs which vary in height from 5cm to 3m and spread from 20cm to 2m, and can be used in the rockery, for ground cover or as specimen plants. All, except the winter and spring flowering types, must have acid soils and all prefer a sunny site. Top dress annually with peat. Leaves needle-like and usually green, but sometimes orange, red or yellow. The bell-shaped flowers are pink, purple, white or bicoloured and carried in terminal sprays at any time of year according to species and varieties. Among winter and spring flowering species are *Erica carnea* (**35**), *E.* x *darleyensis, E. mediterranea*, and their varieties. Summer and autumn flowering species include *E. cinerea, E. terminalis, E. tetralix* and *E. vagans* and their varieties. Propagate by late summer 5-cm side shoot cuttings with heel, rooted in propagating unit, or by layering large plants. Prune by clipping off dead flower heads, and trim large species with shears to prevent straggly growth after flowering. See also **Calluna,** page 59, and **Daboecia,** page 65.

Escallonia S,E,Se
A group of evergreen or semi-evergreen shrubs that grow freely in any garden soil, particularly well in coastal areas. Useful for hedges (set 45cm apart) and wind breaks as well as specimens. Some are not fully hardy and are best sited in a sunny sheltered position. Leaves usually lanceolate or more rounded, and mid to dark green. The flower clusters are carried throughout summer and the tubular blooms are white, pink or red. Height is 1·5 to 3m and spread 1·5 to 2m. The species are not particularly spectacular and the hybrids and varieties raised are most commonly grown. Among these are *Escallonia* x 'Edinensis', (syn. *E.* x *langleyensis*) (Se), and *E.* x *iveyi* (E) and the 'Donard' varieties, also 'C.F. Ball' and 'Apple Blossom' (**36**). Propagation is by 7·5- to 10-cm heel cuttings in late summer in a cold frame. Prune by trimming species and hedges after flowering; cut back hard any straggly branches at the same time.

Eucalyptus T/S,E
Gum Tree
Usually grown as specimen trees when they reach a height of 6 to 20m, according to species, but can be induced to grow in shrub form by pruning back near to the ground one to two years after planting. They have unusual leaves often rounded and silvery blue or bronze when young (juvenile), becoming green and lanceolate as the plants mature. The trees form a lightly branched head and cast dappled shade. The bark of the trunk is often flaky and colourful. White clusters of flowers are produced in summer on plants six years old or more. They prefer a well-drained, moderately rich and chalk-free

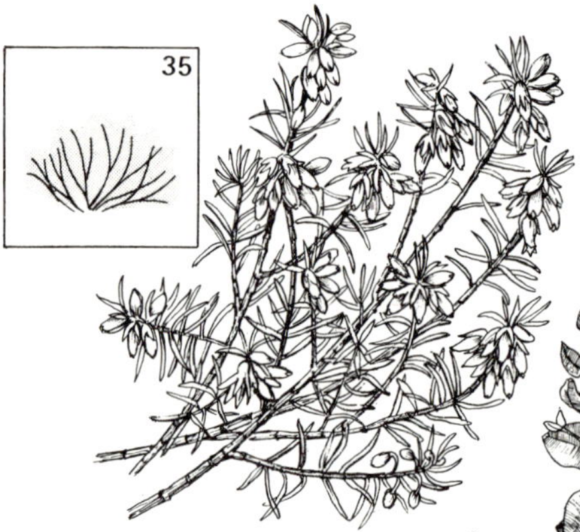

Juvenile foliage

soil in sun but dislike dry conditions. Stake young trees firmly after planting for best results. The hardy species usually grown are *Eucalyptus dalrympleana*, *E. gunnii* (**37**) and *E. niphophila*, growing up to about 12m high and spreading about 5m. Propagate from seed in heat or buy small new plants. Prune in late spring to keep them to the shape required.

Euonymus S,E,D
Spindleberry, Spindle Tree
Shrubs grown mainly for the autumn colour of their ovate leaves and lobed pods with red seeds, they thrive well in all types of soil, including chalk, and by the sea. The evergreen varieties, often with variegated leaves, are best given a warm sheltered position. Plant in clusters to ensure fruiting. Some evergreen species are useful for hedging (planted 45cm apart) and ground cover. Height of deciduous varieties is 1·5 to 3m by a spread of 1 to 2m and good species to plant are *Euonymus alata*, *E. europaeus* and its varieties, and *E. yedoensis*. The recommended evergreens are *E. fortunei* (**38**) and *E. japonica* and their varieties, which vary in height from 30cm to 2m and spread from 30cm to 3m.
Propagation is by 7·5- to 10-cm long heel cuttings in summer in a cold frame. Little pruning is required, except to trim hedges in late spring and early autumn. Cut back hard if necessary in early summer.

38

39

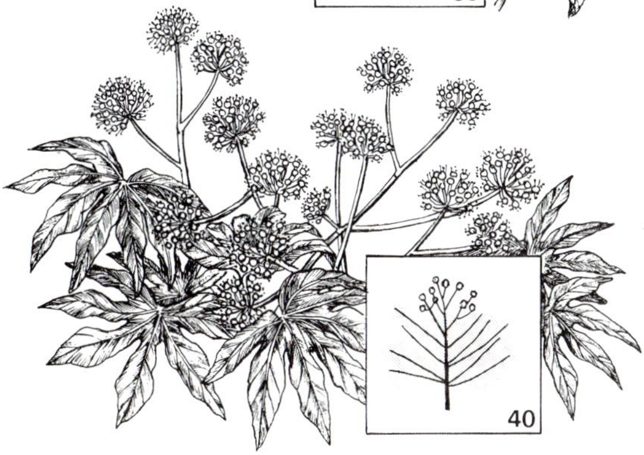
40

Fagus T,D
Beech
Fagus sylvatica (**39**), the common beech, forms a tall tree of rounded shape with bright green ovate leaves turning yellow and brown in autumn. The inconspicuous green flowers are followed by brown fruits in autumn. It is too tall for most gardens, but its varieties, which grow to a height and spread of about 6m or more and have various leaf colours and are rounded to pendulous shapes, make useful specimen trees. If kept clipped, they can be used for hedging, planted 60cm apart. All grow well in any soils. Propagate by seed sown outdoors in early autumn. Prune by trimming trees and hedges as necessary in mid-summer (hedges will retain their russetty leaves throughout winter if pruned in this way).

Fatsia (syn. Aralia) S,E
Castor Oil Plant
Only one species, *Fatsia japonica* (**40**), which grows well in any soil, situation, sun or shade. Exotic looking dark green, palmate shiny leaves and large white heads of flowers in autumn. Height and spread 2 to 4m. Propagate by seeds sown in spring in heat or sucker shoots rooted in a cold frame. Prune only to remove straggly growths.

Forsythia S,D
Golden Bell Bush
This easily-grown hardy shrub is cultivated for its clusters of

yellow, tubular, late winter or early spring flowers that appear before the lanceolate leaves. Height and spread about 2·5m by 2·5m. The most commonly grown are *Forsythia* x *intermedia* (**41**) and *F. suspensa* and their forms, hybrids and varieties. *F.* x *intermedia* 'Spectabilis' is useful for an informal hedge, planted 45cm apart. Propagate by 30-cm cuttings of new wood in autumn or removing naturally rooted layered shoots in autumn. Prune out old wood and cut back flowering shoots after flowering and clip hedges to shape at the same time. Hard prune *F. suspensa* if trained as a wall shrub by cutting back flowered shoots to one or two buds in late spring.

Fuchsia S,D

The hardy fuchsias for growing outdoors are the many varieties of *Fuchsia magellanica* (**42**) and hybrids (from this and other species). This species, which grows up to 3m with a spread of about 2m, is useful as a specimen plant, or for hedging in milder districts, with the plants set 45cm apart. They grow in any good garden soil enriched with humus matter but do not like drought. Sunny or light shady positions are preferable. The leaves are lanceolate, green or variegated, and the pendulous tubular flowers, borne from early summer to autumn, are in shades of red, pink, purple, mauve, white, or bicoloured. The hardy *F. magellanica* varieties vary in height and spread from 60cm to 2m, as do the hardy hybrids. Although usually grown as bushes, some are grown as standards with a bare stem of about 60cm and a rounded head. Propagation is by 7·5- to 10-cm tip cuttings in mild heat spring to autumn. Prune bushes to ground level and cut back shoots of standards in early spring. In exposed areas growth may be killed by frost so also cut dead shoots. Protection may be given to the root area with an autumn mulch of peat or leaves.

Garrya S,E

Silk Tassel Bush

The one species commonly grown is *Garrya elliptica* (**43**) which, with its grey-green ovate leaves and late winter or early spring greeny-yellow, 15-22-cm long, silky catkins, is very showy in a protected position or against a south facing wall. This male form is the only one in general cultivation, and grows about 4m high by 3m wide. It grows well in any soil but dislikes root disturbance. Protect by mulching root area and screening the first winter. Propagate by 7·5- to10-cm heel cuttings in summer in a cold frame or layer in autumn. Prune to remove straggly growths in late spring.

Genista S,D

Broom

Similar to Cytisus, these like a well-drained soil and a sunny position. The leaves are small and lanceolate, or almost non-existent. The yellow pea-shaped flowers, often fragrant, smother the branches in late spring and early summer. The tallest growing species is *Genista aetnensis* with a height and spread of about 5m. Smaller species include *G. hispanica*, *G. lydia* (**44**) and *G. tinctoria* and its forms; these grow to a height and spread of 60cm to 1·2m. All resent root disturbance so they are best planted from pots. Propagate by 5- to 10-cm heel cuttings in summer in a cold frame, or by seeds sown in heat in spring. Prune if necessary after flowering; to keep young plants bushy, cut out growing points of shoots.

Gleditsia (syn. Gleditschia) T,D

Honey Locust

The most usually grown species is *Gleditsia triacanthos* (**45**) and its varieties. Makes a good specimen tree in any soil, growing up to 9m with a spread of 3m. The ornamental leaves are light and pinnate, turning yellow in autumn. The flowers are inconspicuous but are followed by dark brown and twisted seed pods. The trunk and branches are very spiny. Propagation is by seeds sown in a cold frame in spring. Prune only to remove dead wood.

Hamamelis S,D

Witch Hazel

Attractive shrubs which carry their clusters of scented and unusual strap-petalled flowers, yellow, red, or red and yellow, on leafless twiggy branches during winter. The leaves are usually ovate and often colour in autumn. They like a neutral or acid, moist soil in a sunny, sheltered position. They grow to a height and spread of about 3m. Most commonly grown are *Hamamelis* x *intermedia*, *H. japonica* and *H. mollis* (**46**) and their varieties. Propagate by layering in early autumn or 10-cm heel cuttings rooted in a cold frame at the same period. Prune back any straggly shoots after flowering.

Hebe S,E

Veronica

These are very easily grown, evergreen shrubs from New Zealand, which like a sunny position. According to variety they are useful as specimens in a border, for the rockery or as ground cover plants. The leaves

are usually ovate, occasionally lanceolate, and pale or dark green, sometimes grey. Flower spikes are borne in summer and autumn, each bloom being four-petalled, cup-shaped, and in shades of blue, violet, pink or white.
The dwarf and prostrate forms, growing to a height and spread of up to 1m, include *Hebe albicans*, *H.* 'Autumn Glory', *H.* 'Carl Teschner', and *H.* 'Pagei' (syns. *H. pageana* and *H. pinguifolia*). Taller growing specimens with a height and spread of up to 1·5m are *H. brachysiphon* (syn. *H. traversii*), *H.* 'Great Orme' and *H. salicifolia*. Although tender in all except the mildest seaside gardens, *H. speciosa* and its varieties and hybrids (**47**) are particularly colourful.
Propagation is by 5- to 10-cm long cuttings in summer in a cold frame. Pruning is unnecessary except to cut back straggly shoots in late spring.

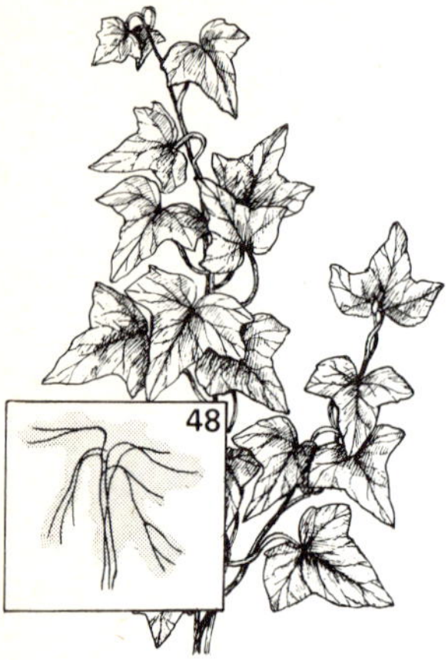

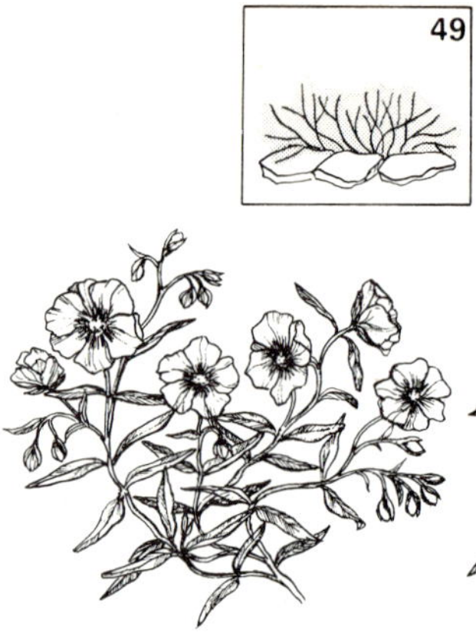

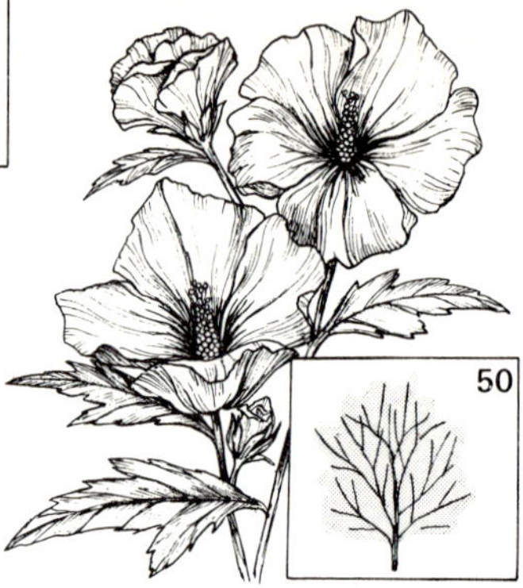

Hedera Cl,E
Ivy
Easily grown hardy foliage climbers for clinging to walls or for use as ground cover in bushy form. They grow freely in any soil, condition or position and survive neglect. The young leaves are usually lobed and the adult ones ovate, sometimes deeply cut; they may be shiny green, yellow or variegated. The green flower and fruit clusters are carried on the top growths but are usually fairly insignificant. The many varieties of *Hedera canariensis*, and *H. helix* (**48**) are most commonly grown and reach a height and spread of 5 to 6m. Propagate by 7·5- to 10-cm tip cuttings in summer in heat; use runner growths for climbers and adult growths for bushy forms. Prune by clipping to shape in early spring and summer.

Helianthemum S,E
Rock Rose, Sun Rose
Small evergreen shrubs which grow well in any soil in a sunny position; particularly useful for rock gardens and dry situations. The linear leaves are green or greyish, and the rather flat flowers are borne in abundance in early summer in a wide variety of colours except blue. Most commonly grown are the varieties of *Helianthemum nummularium* (**49**, syns. *H. chamaecistus*, *H. vulgare*) which reach a height of about 15cm and a spread of 60cm. Propagate by 5-cm long non-flowering side shoots with a heel in summer in a cold frame. Prune by cutting back with shears after flowering. *Note:* helianthemums are sometimes listed in plant catalogues under herbaceous perennials.

Hibiscus S,D
Tree Hollyhock, Tree Mallow
Useful as specimens or in mixed borders with their rounded shape and late summer to early autumn single or double flowers which resemble small hollyhock blooms. The flowers are white, pink, blue, or bicoloured, and saucer shaped. The three lobed leaves are glossy green and appear later in spring than most other shrubs. They like a well drained soil, full sun and shelter from cold winds. The varieties of *Hibiscus syriacus* (**50**) are most usually grown and reach a height of about 3m and a spread of about 2m. Propagation is by 7·5- to 10-cm heel cuttings of non-flowering shoots in summer in heat. Prune long shoots after flowering to maintain the shape.

Hydrangea S,Cl,D
Hydrangea petiolaris (syn. *H. scandens*) is a self clinging climber which can ultimately reach a height and spread of about 18m. It has plate-like clusters of white flowers in early summer and grows well in a north facing position. The other hydrangeas grown outdoors are all deciduous shrubs and prefer a sunny or semi-shaded, protected position. All need a rich well-drained soil, plenty of moisture in summer and the addition of humus-forming matter annually. The leaves are usually broadly ovate sometimes toothed, and generally green. The most popular species grown is *H. macrophylla* (syn. *H. hortensis*). The flowers, of blue, pink, or white, from summer to early autumn, are borne in large mop-head clusters (hortensia

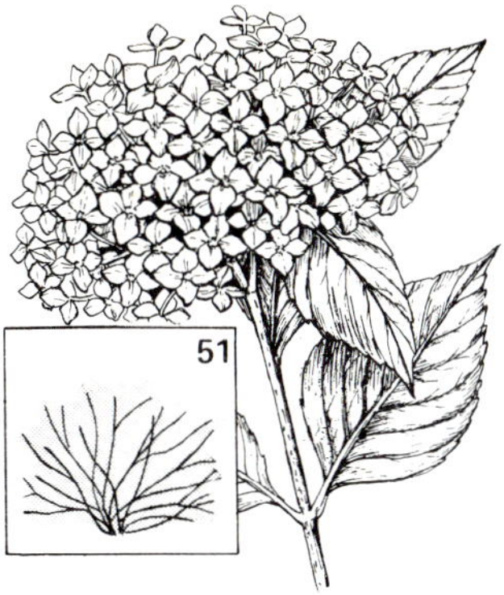

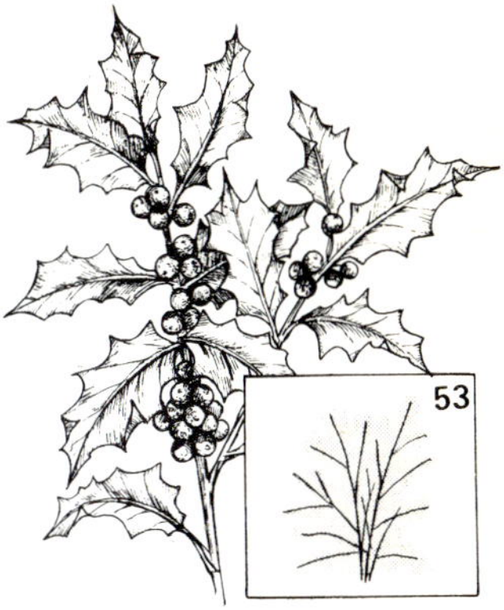

group) or flat heads, about 15cm across (lacecap group). The growth, height and spread of these groups are 1·5 to 2m. On chalky soils, the blue varieties will turn pink unless a bluing powder is applied every 7 to 14 days during the growing season, but they retain their blue colour naturally on acid, peaty soils. Conversely, pink varieties may turn purplish or mauve if grown in acid or neutral soils. Other species grown include *H. paniculata* and its varieties, with white flowers, and *H. villosa*, lavender-blue blooms. Height and spread of these is between 1·5 and 2m. Propagation is by 10-cm cuttings of climbing species in early summer or shrubby species in early autumn, both in a cold frame. Prune by removing old flower heads (which are decorative for flower arrangements) in autumn or mid-spring. Also thin out old wood of *H. macrophylla* varieties (**51**) at ground level and hard prune *H. paniculata* in spring. If grown in an exposed position, young growths may be killed by spring frosts, so give protection.

Hypericum S,E,D,Se
St. John's Wort, Rose of Sharon
Some are useful for ground cover, others as specimens in the border, and the dwarf forms in rockeries. The green leaves are ovate or lanceolate, many of the species evergreen and some of the deciduous species semi-evergreen in mild climates and giving autumn colour tints. The flowers are single, saucer-shaped and bright yellow, and appear from early summer to autumn; in some cases they are followed by red fruits. All will grow in any soil and thrive in full sun. Shrubby species for the border include *Hypericum androsaemum* (D), *H. elatum* (Se), *H. patulum* (Se) and its forms, including *H.p.* 'Hidcote' (Se). All grow to a height and spread of 1 to 2m. Low growing species include *H. calycinum* (**52**) (E) and *H.* x *moserianum* (Se), reaching a height of about 30 to 60cm and an indefinite spread. Propagate by 5- to 10-cm cuttings in a cold frame in summer, or division of *H. calycinum* in autumn. Prune the taller shrubs almost to ground level in spring and trim the low growing species also.

Ilex T,S,E
Holly
As very slow growing, usually treated as shrub rather than tree, forming a pyramidal shape. Grows well in any soil, in sun or shade, though the variegated leaf forms do best in sun. The leaves are ovate, usually prickly and are shiny dark green, yellow, silver or variegated. The early summer white or green flowers are inconspicuous but are followed by red berries on the female plants, provided both males and females are planted together. The male forms do not berry but are grown for their foliage. Ultimate height can be up to 8m and spread up to 4m, but in gardens they rarely achieve these proportions. Good species, hybrids and their varieties to grow include *Ilex* x *altaclarensis* and *I. aquifolium* (**53**), also the smaller *I. crenata* and *I. pernyii* varieties. Most make good hedging plants set 60cm apart. Propagation is by 7·5- to 10-cm heel cuttings in summer in a cold frame. Prune specimen trees in summer to maintain shape and trim hedges in spring. Remove green leaved shoots from variegated forms.

Jasminum Cl,D,Se
Jasmine
Very popular plants for climbing and training against walls, over trellis, pergolas, old trees and such like. They grow well in any soil in a sunny position, preferably protected from cold winds. The leaves are generally pinnate and the yellow, white or pink flowers trumpet-shaped in clusters and usually fragrant. Height and spread are between 3 and 9m, according to training of the plants. The earliest to flower, from winter to spring, is *Jasminum nudiflorum*, followed in summer by *J. officinale* (**54**) and its varieties, and *J.* x *stephanense*. Propagate by 7·5- to 10-cm nodal cuttings in summer in a cold frame, or layering in autumn. Prune to thin out unwanted shoots after flowering.

Juniperus C,T,S,E
Juniper
A genus consisting of large trees of conical to drooping-shape to small, slow-growing, tree-shaped or prostrate species. All grow in any soil, including chalk, and can be used either as specimens in the garden or in tubs, for ground cover or in the rockery and give colour all year round. The leaves may be juvenile, i.e. awl-shaped, or adult with scales; sometimes both are borne at the same time. The colour of the foliage may be green, golden, blue-grey or almost white. Instead of cones fleshy-black or blue berries are produced. Of the tree species *Juniperus chinensis*, *J. communis* (**55**) and *J. virginiana* are most commonly grown and ultimately reach a height of about 8m and a spread of about 2m. There are very many dwarf varieties of these and other species, including *J. horizontalis*, *J. procumbens*, *J. sabina* and *J. squamata*. Height and spread are approximately 60cm to 2m by 2m in most dwarf forms including the popular grey-blue 'tree' 'Skyrocket'. Propagate by seeds or 5- to 10-cm heel cuttings in autumn, both in a cold frame. Pruning consists of removing unwanted shoots of small varieties in spring or summer.

Kalmia S,E
Sheep Laurel, Calico Bush
Hardy plants for any chalk-free soil in sun or light shade. They bear lanceolate leathery green leaves, and a mass of clusters of pink saucer-shaped flowers in early summer. The most commonly grown species is *Kalmia latifolia* (**56**) with a height and spread of 2 to 3m. Propagate by layering, or 10-cm cuttings in late summer in a cold frame. Prune only to shape and remove dead flower heads.

Kerria S,D
Jew's Mallow
Only one species, *Kerria japonica* (**57**) and its varieties are commonly grown, either in the border or against walls. They like a well-drained soil and sun or semi-shade. They have slender, glossy green branches and light green or variegated lanceolate, toothed leaves and vary in height and spread from

80cm to 4m. The yellow flowers are single or double and are carried profusely in sprays in late spring. Propagate by 10- to 12·5-cm cuttings in late summer in a cold frame, or division during winter. Prune back all flowered shoots in early summer to new growths, and cut out old wood.

Laburnum T/S,D
Golden Rain, Golden Chain
Trained as trees or shrubs these make attractive graceful specimens for the garden. They grow well in any soil, in sun or light shade, but should be staked until established. Long, dense yellow sprays of pea-shaped flowers are carried in early summer. The leaves are green or yellow and compound with three lanceolate leaflets. The flowers are followed by brown bean-like seed pods. In winter the young shoots are shiny green. *Laburnum alpinum*, *L. anagyroides* (**58**, syn. *L. vulgare*) and *L.* x *watereri* (syn. *L.* x *vossii*) are most usually grown. Height is up to 6m and spread up to 4m. Propagation is by seeds sown in a cold frame in early autumn. No pruning is required. *Note:* all parts of the plant are poisonous, especially the seeds. Some catalogues list *L. adamii*, with pink, yellow and purple flowers all on the same tree. This is a graft hybrid between *Laburnum anagyroides* and *Cytisus purpureus* and should correctly be listed as X *Laburnocytisus adamii*.

Laurus S,E
Bay Laurel, Sweet Bay
Hardy in a sunny position for growing in the garden or in containers (sometimes trained as small standards). Does well in any soil. Mature height and spread up to 6m. Leaves are lanceolate and shiny green, aromatic when crushed and used in cooking. Inconspicuous green flowers are borne in clusters in late spring and the female forms produce black berries. *Laurus nobilis* (**59**) is usually grown. Propagate by 10-cm heel cuttings in late summer in a cold frame, or layering in summer. Prune by cutting to shape as necessary once or twice during summer.

Lavandula S,E
Lavender
These are popular aromatic shrubs grown as specimens or low hedges, by setting the plants about 30cm apart. They grow best in any well-drained soil in a sunny position. The stems are grey, as are the linear leaves, and the spikes of tubular flowers in shades of purple, blue, violet or white are carried throughout the summer. The dried flowers can be used for indoor decoration, 'lavender bags' or *pot pourris*. The two species grown are *Lavandula spica* (**60**, Old English Lavender) and *L. vera* (Dutch Lavender) and their varieties. Height and spread are between 60cm and 1·2m. Propagation is by 7·5- to 10-cm cuttings in late summer in a cold frame. Prune by trimming to shape after flowering or clip back in spring.

Ligustrum S,E,Se
Privet
Particularly useful for hedges (set 30 to 45cm apart) and specimen plants, they grow well in ordinary soil and any position. Growth is compact with the leaves ovate and dark green, golden-yellow or variegated on certain forms. The flowers are white, and are carried in upright panicles during summer and early autumn. Height is up to 5m and spread about 2m. Species in general cultivation are *Ligustrum japonicum* (E), *L. lucidum* (E) and *L. ovalifolium* (**61**, Se) and their varieties. Propagate by 10- to 15-cm cuttings in autumn in a cold frame. Prune by clipping hedges or specimens to the required height and shape in early summer and early autumn.

Lonicera S,Cl,E,D,Se
Honeysuckle
This genus has a wide variety of uses; the shrubs for borders or hedging (e.g. *Lonicera nitida*, set about 30cm apart), and the climbers for twining up supports or training against walls and fences. All like ordinary soil preferably containing humus matter for the climbers. The shrubs do best in full sun but the climbers in light shade. The leaves are usually ovate and various shades of green or occasionally yellow. The flowers, appearing at different times of year according to species and varieties, are tubular, borne in pairs or clusters, are often fragrant and are yellow, red, orange, or white. Good shrubby species to choose include *Lonicera frangrantissima* (Se), winter flowering, and *L. nitida* (E) and *L. pileata* (E), both late spring flowering, followed by berries. Height and spread vary from 60cm to 1·5m.

Climbing species and hybrids most commonly grown and flowering in summer are *L.* x *americana* (syn. *L. grata*) (D), *L. japonica* (Se), *L. periclymenum* (**62**, D) and *L.* x *tellmanniana* (D) and their varieties. Ultimate height can be 10m and spread is according to area allotted. Propagation by 20- to 30-cm hardwood cuttings in the open in autumn, layering in autumn, or seeds sown in a cold frame. Prune hedges and shrubs two or three times yearly during summer to encourage shape and bushy growth, and cut out old wood and thin climbers as necessary in autumn.

Magnolia T,S,E,D
Tulip Tree, Lily Tree
Magnificent trees and shrubs producing spectacular large flowers in late spring, sometimes followed by cone-like fruits. All need a sunny sheltered position in well-drained chalk-free soil, and due to shallow rooting, benefit from annual mulching and not being underplanted. The leaves are shiny or mat green, ovate or lanceolate, and often downy beneath. The flowers are bowl or star-shaped, usually fragrant, and pink, white or bicoloured. With the exception of *Magnolia grandiflora*, which is evergreen, the others usually grown are deciduous. These latter include *M. denudata* (syn. *M. conspicua*), *M. kobus*, *M.*

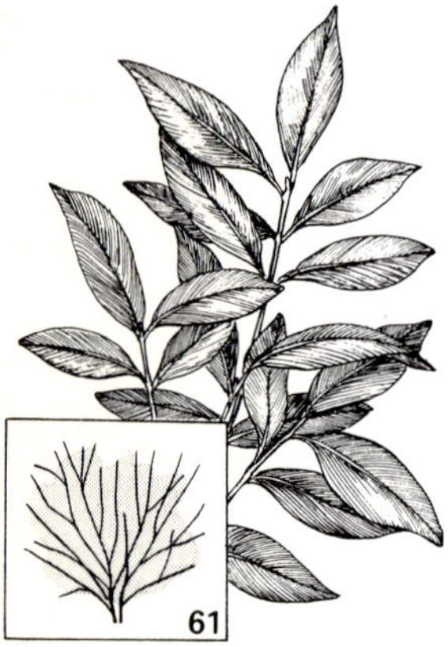
61

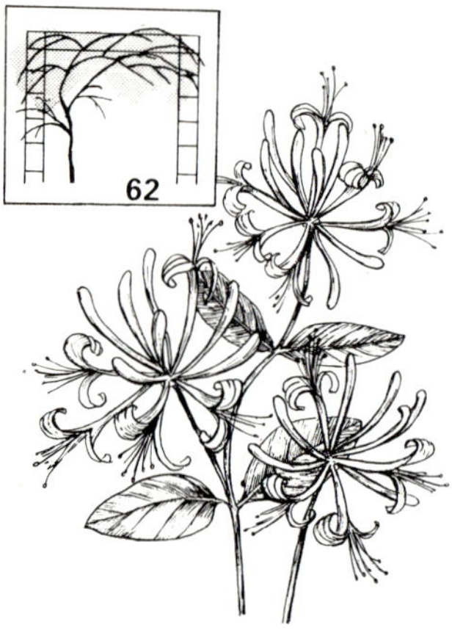
62

63

liliiflora, *M.* x *loebneri*, *M. sieboldii* (syn. *M. parviflora*), *M.* x *soulangiana* (**63**) and *M. stellata* and their varieties. Height and spread vary according to growing conditions but can be up to 4m by 4m. Propagate by seeds in a cold frame in autumn, layering in spring, or 10-cm heel cuttings in summer in heat. No pruning is required, except if grown against a wall when trained to shape in late spring.

Mahonia S,E

Excellent evergreen shrubs, as specimens or for ground cover, which grow well in any free-draining soil in shade. The leaves are usually dark green, compound and prickly, sometimes colouring in autumn. The flowers are yellow and borne in dense sprays in late winter; many are fragrant and some produce autumn berries. Good forms to grow include *Mahonia aquifolium*, *M.* x 'Charity', *M. japonica* (syn. *M. bealei*), *M. lomariifolia* (**64**) and *M. pinnata*. The average height is 1 to 3m and the spread about 2m. Propagation is by seeds sown in late summer in a cold frame, or 7·5- to 10-cm cuttings in mid-summer in heat. Pruning is unnecessary unless used as ground cover, when cut back as required in late spring.

Malus T,D

Crab Apple, Flowering Crab

Flowering and ornamental fruit-bearing trees which include the parents of modern apples. Although grown mainly for decorative purposes as specimens, their green, yellow or red fruits can be cooked or made into preserves. The leaves are usually ovate and mid-green or bronze and the spring flowers, slightly fragrant, borne in clusters in shades of pink, red, white or bicoloured. Height and spread vary from 4 to 7m. All like any soil with humus added, and prefer sunny or lightly shaded positions. To ensure fruits, plant more than one tree for cross pollination. Although there are a number of species still grown, such as *Malus floribunda*, *M. hupehensis* (syn. *M. theifera*), and *M. sargentii*, many have been superseded by hybrids and varieties which include *M.* 'Dartmouth', *M.* 'Echtermeyer', *M.* x *eleyi*, *M.* 'Golden Hornet', *M.* 'John Downie' (**65**), *M.* 'Katherine', *M.* x *lemoinei* and *M.* 'Profusion'. Propagation is by budding or grafting, which is not easy, so new plants are best purchased. Once formed to the required shape, prune only to remove dead and straggly shoots; this is best carried out in late winter.

Olearia S,E

Daisy Bush

Excellent for coastal gardens or sheltered positions inland, they grow best in any well-drained soil in sun. The leaves are ovate, lanceolate or sometimes holly-like and vary from green to grey, often white and woolly beneath. The daisy-like flowers are white and borne profusely in clusters in summer. The height and spread vary from 1 to 3m. Popular forms are *Olearia haastii*, *O. Macrodonta* (**66**) and *O.* x *scilloniensis*. Propagate by 10-cm side shoot cuttings in

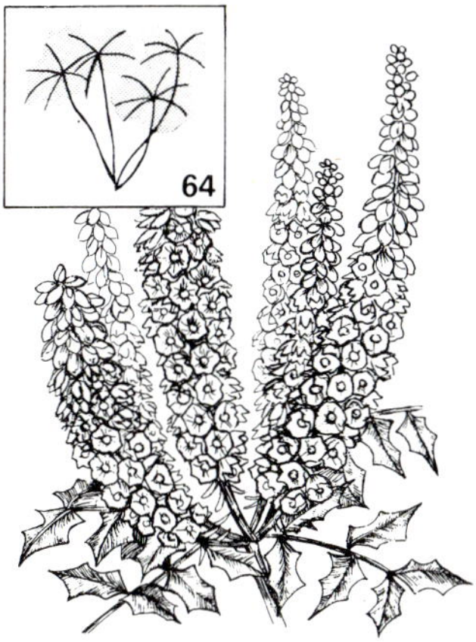

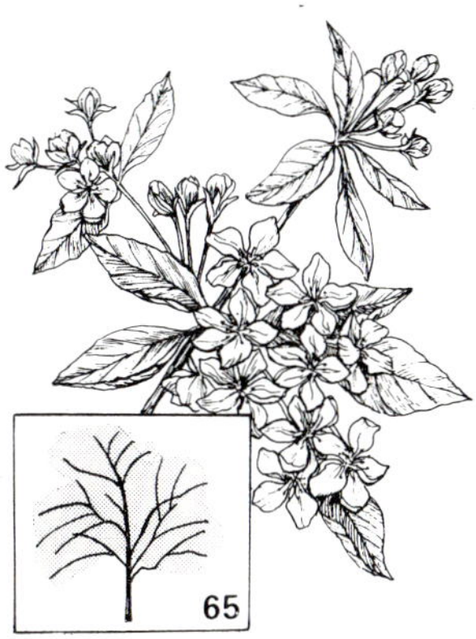

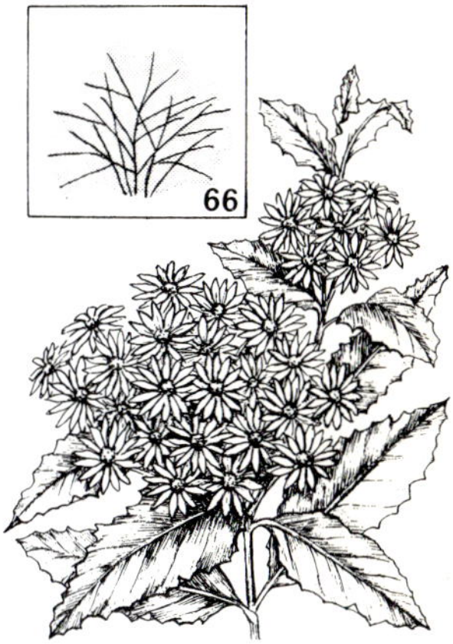

summer in a cold frame. Prune to remove dead shoots in late spring.

Osmanthus S,E

Slow growing specimen shrubs to plant in well-drained soil in sun or light shade. The leaves are usually ovate and spiny, sometimes holly-like. The flowers are white, tubular, scented and in dense clusters, borne on *Osmanthus delavayi* (**67**) in late spring and on *O. heterophyllus* (syns. *O. aquifolius* and *O. ilicifolius*) in early autumn. These are the only two species in common cultivation. The height and spread of both is 2 to 3m. Propagate by 10-cm cuttings in mid-summer in heat or by layering in autumn. No pruning is necessary, except to clip *O. heterophyllus* in late spring if used as a hedge, with the plants set 45cm apart.

Paeonia S,D

Tree Paeony (or Peony)

Although most paeonies are herbaceous perennials, there are several shrub forms useful as border specimens. The green leaves are compound, with irregularly-shaped leaflets, and the flowers, produced in late spring, are bowl-shaped in shades of yellow, red, or white, single or semi-double. The two species and their varieties most commonly grown are *Paeonia lutea* (**68**) and *P. suffruticosa* (syn. *P. moutan*). They prefer rich, deep soil and protection of other shrubs against early morning sun which might damage any frosted blooms. Height and spread is between 1 and 2m. Propagate by layering in spring, carefully removing and replacing rooted suckers in autumn, or 15- to 20-cm cuttings in late autumn in a cold frame. Prune to remove dead wood in spring.

Parthenocissus (syn. Ampelopsis) Cl,D

Virginia Creeper

Grown particularly for their attractive leaves and ability to climb up supports by means of tendrils with sticky discs. The leaves are compound, usually three or five lobed and are green, sometimes with the veins lined pink and silver, and all produce rich red autumn colours. The early summer flowers are insignificant. They like a rich, moist, free draining soil and plenty of humus matter. Support young growths until the plant is established. Three species worth growing are *Parthenocissus henryana* (syn. *Vitis henryana*), *P. quinquefolia* (**69**, syn. *Vitis hederacea*), and *P. tricuspidata* (syns. *Ampelopsis veitchii* and *Vitis inconstans*). Height and spread are about 4 to 6m. Propagate by 10- to 12·5-cm nodal cuttings in late summer in heat, or by layering long shoots in autumn. Prune to remove unwanted shoots during summer.

Pernettya S,E

Prickly Heath

Shrubs grown primarily for their colourful fruits which last well throughout winter. They do best in a chalk-free peaty soil with plenty of humus, and fruit best in sunny positions. They make excellent ground cover plants, having a height and spread up to about 60 to 90cm. Small, dark green leaves cover often red stems and the heather-like, bell-shaped flowers are produced in early summer. The fruits are born in clusters and can be white, red, purple, mauve or pink. To ensure berrying, male and female forms should be planted together in clumps. The only species grown is *Pernettya mucronata* (**70**), but it has numerous named forms.

Propagate by 5-cm cuttings or seeds in autumn in a cold frame. Prune to keep to shape and remove old wood in late winter.

Philadelphus S,D

Mock Orange

Grown for their freedom of flowering in early summer and attractive ovate, vein marked, green leaves. The flowers are usually white, single or double, and carried in profuse clusters; they have a strong scent of orange blossom. They like a well-drained soil in sun or partial shade. Average height and spread is 2m by 1·5m though *Philadelphus microphyllus* is about 80cm by 80cm. Most usually grown are the hybrids such as *P.* 'Beauclerk', *P.* 'Belle Etoile' *P.* 'Sybille' and *P.* 'Virginal' (**71**). Propagate by 10-cm cuttings in late summer in a cold frame. Prune out old wood after flowering.

Picea C.T.E

Spruce, Fir

Mainly tall pyramid-shaped trees, many with pendulous branches, going up to about 18m, but also a number of dwarf slow-growing forms, growing about 3·5m by 1·5m or less. The green, blue or greyish leaves are usually needle-like, the bark rough, and brown drooping cones are generally produced annually. The trees make useful screens, specimens or rock garden plants. The species most commonly grown include *Picea abies* (syn. *P. excelsa*), the Christmas Tree, *P. glauca* (**72**), *P. mariana*, *P. omorika*, *P. pungens* and *P. sitchensis* and their dwarf forms. They all grow well in deep, moist soil, but dislike chalk, and like a sunny or semi-shaded position. Propagation is by seeds in spring in a cold frame, but this is difficult so it is best to buy new

67

70

71

68

72

69

73

plants. No pruning is required except to remove forked shoots to leave one main growth.

Pieris (syn. Andromeda) S,E
Excellent specimen shrubs which grow well in any chalk-free, moist soil in light shade. They like annual mulching. The evergreen shiny leaves are ovate or lanceolate, green or red in spring, and the panicles of urn-shaped white flowers are borne in profusion from mid- to late spring. *Pieris floribunda*, *P. forrestii* (**73**) and *P. japonica*, and the varieties of the last two, are most often grown. They vary in height from 1 to 2m and spread from 60cm to 1·5m. Propagation is by 7·5- to 10-cm cuttings in summer in a cold frame or seeds sown in winter in a cold frame. Prune by removing the dead flower heads and any straggly shoots in early summer.

Pinus C,T,E
Pine
Most pines are too large for all except the big gardens as they grow up to 20m or more, but there are several smaller species and forms which are useful as specimens or in the rock or heather garden. The leaves are in groups of 'needles' which are green, blue-green or grey-green. The cones are usually brown and scaley, either round or cylindrical. They like a rich well-drained soil, preferably without chalk, and do best in sunny positions. Good species to grow include *Pinus aristata*, *P. mugo*, *P. nigra*, *P. sylvestris* and *P. wallichiana* (**74**, syns. *P. excelsa* and *P. griffithii*) and their dwarf forms. The height and spread of the taller forms will be up to 10m by 5m, and the dwarf forms about 3m by 2m. Propagation, by seeds in spring in a cold frame, is difficult so it is best to buy new plants. Prune only to maintain one leading shoot.

Polygonum Cl,D
Russian Vine, Mile a Minute
Although most Polygonums are hardy annuals or perennials, *Polygonum baldschuanicum* (**75**) is a fast-growing climbing species and excellent for covering eyesores. If grown against a wall it requires trellis or wires. It thrives in any soil and any position and will grow as much as 4 to 5m per year, ultimately reaching 12m or more. The leaves are ovate and pale green. The white, pink tinged flowers are borne in sprays in profusion throughout summer and early autumn. Propagate by 10-cm heel cuttings in late autumn in the open. Prune back hard in spring to retain the required spread and height and prevent straggly growth.

Potentilla S,D
Cinquefoil
Although many Potentillas are annuals or perennials, the small shrubby species are very popular for their long flowering period, from early summer to mid-autumn. The twiggy stems carry small green or silvery-grey, deeply cut leaves, and the flowers, white, yellow or red, are similar to tiny single roses. All like a well-drained soil, preferably in full sun. Their height and spread vary from 30cm to 1·5m. Most usually grown are the many varieties of *Potentilla fruticosa* (**76**). Propagation by 7·5-cm heel cuttings in late autumn in a cold frame. Prune to remove dead heads after flowering and keep bushy by cutting out old wood at ground level in spring.

Prunus T,S,D,E
Flowering Almonds (D), Apricots (D), Cherries (D), Peaches (D), Plums (D), Cherry Laurels (E)
A very large genus containing some of the most popular ornamental spring flowering trees and shrubs as well as evergreen laurels for all-year-round attraction. All like a well-drained soil, preferably with some chalk, and a sunny position, though the laurels will grow well in light shade and can be used for hedges or screens if planted about 60cm apart. The leaves are either lanceolate or

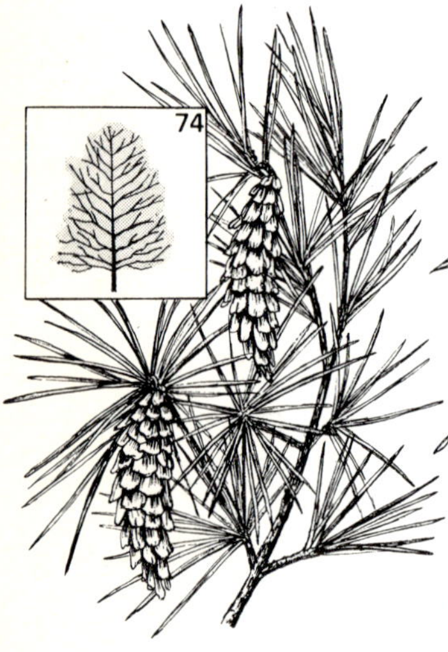

ovate and green or red; with some species bright autumn colours are produced. The flowers are bowl-shaped, single or double, often fragrant, borne in clusters or sprays and are red, pink, white or bicoloured; in some forms they have ornamental autumn fruits. If grown as trees they mature at a height and spread of about 7m by 5m, or as bushes reach about 4m by 2·5m. The most usually grown almonds are *Prunus* x *amygdalo-persica* 'Pollardii' and *P. amygdalus* (syns. *P. communis* and *P. dulcis*) and their forms; and of apricots, *P. mume* and *P. triloba* (**77**). There are vast numbers of cherries from which to choose, including species such as *P. avium*, *P. padus*, *P. serrula*, *P. serrulata* and *P. subhirtella* (some forms of which flower during winter). Many of the most popular cherries are hybrids or varieties, many of them with Japanese names such as 'Ama no Gawa', 'Kanzan', and 'Shirofugen'. Of the peaches, *P. davidiana* and *P. persica* and their forms are best. Plums include the species, hybrids and varieties of *P.* x *blireiana*, *P. cerasifera* and *P. spinosa* (Sloe). The evergreen cherry laurels are usually the species *P. laurocerasus* and *P. lusitanica* and their varieties. Propagation of most prunus species is difficult and it is advisable to buy new plants. Pruning is generally unnecessary except to maintain shape and remove dead wood; this is best done in late summer. Laurels grown as hedges should be pruned to shape, and specimens cut back, in late spring.

Pyracantha S,E
Firethorn
Can be used as specimens but also for training up walls, against wires or trellis, and for hedging, set about 60cm apart. Very popular for their green, sometimes greyish, oblong leaves, clusters of hawthorn-like white flowers in spring, and long-lived autumn and winter clusters of red or yellow berries. They grow well in any well-drained soil, in sun or light shade. Popular species, hybrids and varieties to grow include *Pyracantha angustifolia*, *P. atalantioides* (syn. *P. gibbsii*), *P. coccinea* (**78**), *P. crenulata* (syn. *P.c.* 'Rogersiana') and *P.* x 'Watereri'. All have spiny branches and reach a height and spread of about 3m. Propagate by 10-cm cuttings in summer in heat or seeds in autumn in a cold frame. Pruning is unnecessary for specimens, but remove unwanted shoots from wall trained shrubs and clip hedges to shape in early summer.

Pyrus T,D
Flowering Pear
The ovate or lanceolate leaves of green or silvery-grey, often colouring in autumn, and the clusters of white flowers in spring, make these attractive specimen trees. They grow to about 6m tall and wide, and like a good, well-drained soil and a sunny position. Commonly grown are *Pyrus calleryana* and *P. salicifolia* (**79**). Propagation is difficult so it is best to buy new plants. Pruning is usually unnecessary, but thin out dead or unwanted growth.

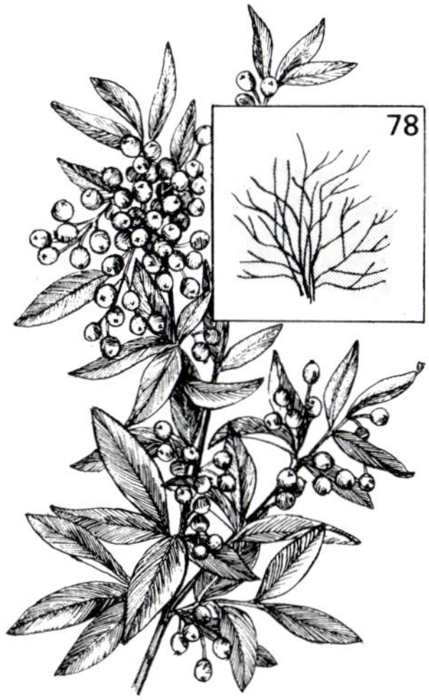

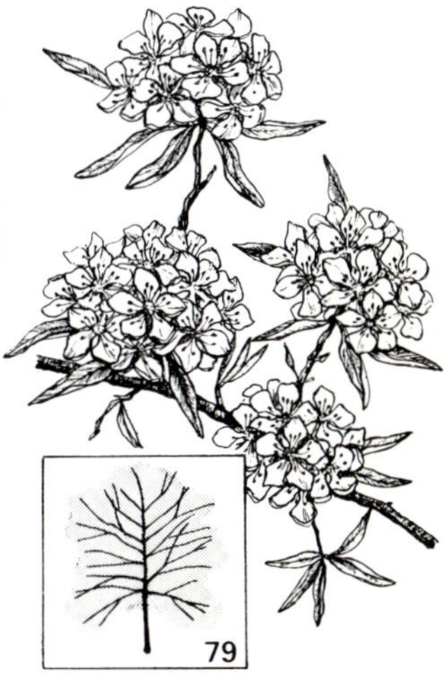

Rhododendron T,S,E,D,Se
Includes Azalea
This is one of the most popular genera for providing flowers from early spring to early summer, and in mild districts the flowering period extends into winter and mid-summer according to the species or variety. The plants vary in shape from tall rambling specimens with a height and spread of up to 12m by 9m down to compact little miniatures of about 30cm by 30cm; most have a height and spread of 1 to 3m. This means there are forms available for growing as trees, specimen shrubs, in a woodland area, for mass plantings, in the rockery, or the heather garden, in mixed borders, in containers, and as informal barriers and hedges (*Rhododendron ponticum* in particular, set 90cm apart). All have large or small lanceolate leaves, mainly green, though sometimes reddish, silvery or with a brown 'felt' undersurface, and the deciduous forms often produce good autumn colour. The flowers, generally borne in clusters, though occasionally single, are usually funnel-shaped and in every shade of colour except true blue; sometimes they are speckled or bicoloured. All rhododendrons must have chalk-free well-drained but moist soil and should be mulched annually with peat or shredded bark. They prefer lightly shaded, wind sheltered positions, where sun will not affect any frosted blooms in the early morning. Most are completely hardy, but some are slightly tender and these are best given the shelter of other plants or protected in winter. The very tender are grown in the greenhouse. Where a soil is not sufficiently acid, it is possible to create a special rhododendron area by

importing suitable soil and watering regularly with a special compound called Sequestrene.

Rhododendrons are a complex and very extensive genus botanically and are usually divided broadly into five groups; rhododendron and azalea species, rhododendron hybrids, azaleodendrons (semi-evergreen hybrids between deciduous azaleas and evergreen rhododendrons), deciduous azalea hybrids, and evergreen azalea hybrids.

There are scores of fine rhododendron and azalea species including *R. augustinii*, *R. concatenans*, *R. discolor*, *R. luteum* (**80**), *R. obiculare*, *R. pemakoense*, *R.racemosum*, *R. russatum*, *R. schlippenbachii*, *R. thomsonii*, and *R. yakushimanum*. Among the popular rhododendron hybrids are 'Azor', 'Betty Wormald', 'Britannia', 'Fastuosum Flore Pleno', 'Goldsworth Orange', 'Loderi', 'May Day', 'Nimbus', 'Pink Pearl' (**81**), 'Purple Splendour', 'Susan', 'Unique' and 'White Swan'. Good azaleodendrons include 'Fragrans' and 'Glory of Littleworth'. In the deciduous azalea section are many forms of the Ghent, *R. mollis*, *R. occidentale*, Exbury and Knap Hill hybrids. The evergreen (or Japanese) azalea hybrids come from strains of *R.* x *malvatica*, *R. kaempferi*, Vuyk, *R. indicum*, *R. amoenum* and Kurume types. In most instances the hybrids have superseded the species and new introductions are made annually, so consult a good catalogue or garden centre before making a final selection. Propagate by layering at any time of year, or by cuttings, grafting and seed but it is best to buy new plants. Cut to shape if necessary after flowering. Always remove dead flower heads.

Rhus T,S,D
Sumach
Sometimes confused with cotinus (see page 63), two easily-grown species, *Rhus glabra* and *R. typhina* (**82**), are usually planted for their brilliant autumn leaf colour. The long green leaves are pinnate, or fern-like in the *R.* 'Laciniata' varieties, and the long spikes of small female flowers are deep pink. Both grow to a height and spread of about 3 to 4m, *R. typhina* being the larger of the two. They grow in any well-drained soil but colour best in a sunny position. Propagation is by 10- to 12·5-cm summer heel cuttings in heat, planting of suckers removed in autumn, or shoots layered in spring. Pruning is not essential but cutting back in late winter improves the foliage effect.

Ribes S,D,E,Se
Flowering Currant, Flowering Gooseberry
Spring flowering shrubs which are popular as specimens or for hedging (*Ribes alpinum* set 30 to 40cm apart). The leaves are ovate and often deeply lobed and in some species colour well in autumn. The flowers, like small fuchsias, are borne in erect or pendulous sprays or clusters, and are yellow, pink or red. If both male and female forms are grown, red, black or blue-black berries are produced in autumn. All grow well in a free-draining soil in sun or light shade. Good species to grow include *R. alpinum* (D), *R. aureum* (syn. *R. odoratum*) (D), *R. laurifolium* (E), *R. sanguineum* (**83**, D) and its varieties, and *R. speciosum* (Se). Height and spread are between 1·5 and 2m. Propagation is by 30-cm long late autumn cuttings in the open. Prune by cutting out old wood after flowering.

Robinia T,S,D
False Acacia
Excellent for sunny positions as specimens or mixed with other trees and shrubs, they do well in any soil. The green or yellow leaves are compound with lanceolate leaflets and the pea-like flowers of pink or white are borne in pendulous sprays in early summer. *Robinia hispida*, *R. kelseyi*, *R. pseudoacacia* (**84**) and *R.p.* 'Frisia' are most usually grown. Propagate by seeds in a cold frame in spring, removing suckers during winter, or grafting 'Frisia'. Pruning is rarely required.

Rosa S,Cl,D,Se
Rose
Roses are among the most popular of all flowering shrubs and climbers. They can be grown on their own, used in mixed borders, planted as barriers or hedges, trained as specimen standards, form a colourful screen against buildings and up wires and trellis, or be planted in rockeries and containers. All have compound leaves, usually five-lobed and toothed, which are sometimes semi-evergreen and produce autumn tints. The flowers, which appear in summer through to late autumn, may be single or double, sometimes fragrant, and borne singly or in clusters in almost every colour variation, or mixture of colours, except true blue. In some species (e.g. *Rosa moyesii* (**85a**), *R. rubrifolia* and *R. rugosa*) brightly coloured fruits (hips) add colour through autumn and winter. Usually the stem growths are thorny or prickly. All like a rich, moist but well drained soil and a sunny position sheltered from strong winds.

The genus Rosa is highly complex and is divided into a number of sections. Most

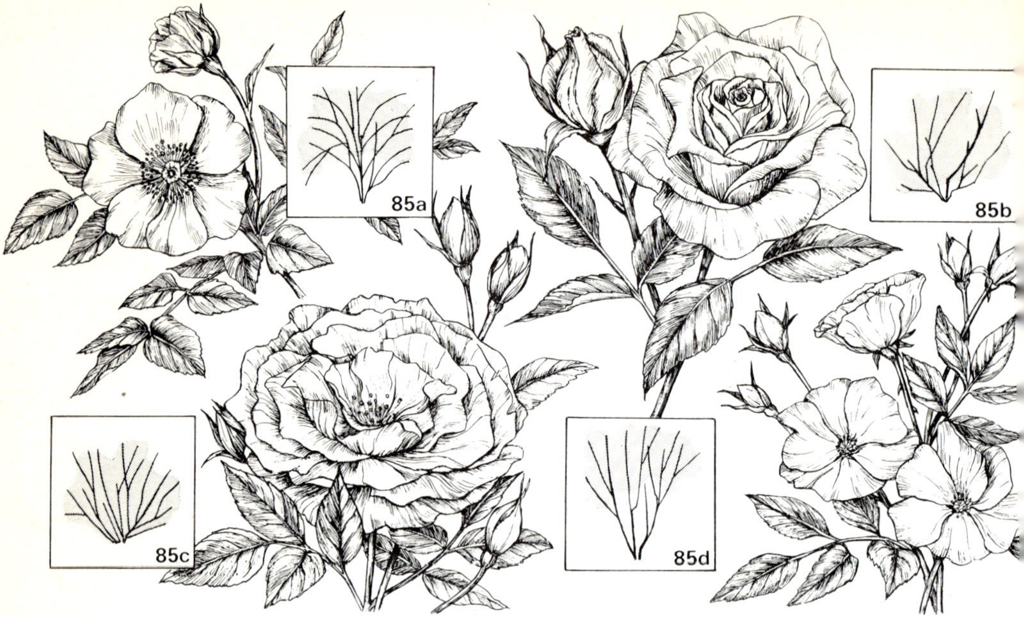

commonly grown today are the formal modern bush roses, which may be hybrid teas (h.t.s **85b**) or floribundas (fl. **85c**). Very many of these are introduced each year, but among just some of the most popular hybrid teas are 'Peace', 'Grandpa Dickson', 'Red Devil', 'Fragrant Cloud', 'Rose Gaujard', 'Wendy Cussons', 'Admiral Rodney', 'Bobby Charlton', 'Ena Harkness', 'Blue Moon', 'Piccadilly', 'Doris Tysterman', 'Bonsoir' and 'Whisky Mac'. Some popular floribundas are 'Korresia', 'Glenfiddich', 'Iceberg', 'Queen Elizabeth', 'Allgold', 'Elizabeth of Glamis', 'Pink Parfait', 'Dorothy Wheatcroft', 'City of Leeds', 'Anne Cocker', 'Escapade', 'Masquerade' and 'Evelyn Fison'. These grow to a height and spread of 1 to 1·5m. The modern miniature bush roses, growing from 15 to 45cm high, include varieties such as 'Baby Masquerade', 'Starina', 'Angela Rippon' ('Ocara-Ocarina'), 'Cinderella' 'New Penny', 'Royal Salute', and 'Darling Flame'. A number of these bush roses may be obtained as standards, with the flowering growths borne at the top of a bare 1m or so high single stem.

Climbing and rambling roses (**85d**) are generally grouped together and many of them are repeat flowering from summer to early autumn. The essential difference between the two is that ramblers have laxer more drooping stems than the climbers, which have fewer shoots from the base and stiffer growth. Some good varieties to grow are 'Alberic Barbier', 'Albertine', 'American Pillar', 'Danse du Feu', 'Golden Showers', 'Handel', Maigold', 'Mermaid', 'New Dawn' and 'Zephirine Drouhin'. These will grow up to about 6m and spread as far as permitted.

The last major group of roses is the shrubs, sub-divided into the species, old-fashioned and modern. The main species types are *R.* x *alba*, *R.* x *borboniana* (Bourbon Roses), *R.* x *centifolia* (Cabbage and Moss Roses), *R. chinensis* (China Roses), *R. damascena* (Damask Roses), *R. gallica* (French Rose) and *R. rugosa*. Among the old fashioned shrub roses (mainly raised in the last century) are hybrids and varieties of the species, such as 'Boule de Neige', 'Celestial', 'Cecile Brunner', 'Perle d'Or', 'Omar Khayyam', 'Canary Bird', 'Souvenir de la Malmaison', 'Blanc Double de Coubert' and 'Frau Dagmar Hastrup'. Most of these grow between 1·5m and 2m high and spread 1 to 1·5m. Twentieth-century modern hybrid shrub roses include 'Elmshorn', 'Fruhlingsgold', 'Golden Wings', 'Marguerite Hilling', 'Nevada', 'The Fairy', and 'Yesterday'. They grow about 2m by 1·5m and make good ornamental hedges set 1m apart. Propagate by 20- to 30-cm heel

cuttings in autumn in the open or buy new plants. For pruning see pages 37 and 39.
Note: a new classification of roses is gradually being introduced and catalogues may alter sections accordingly.

Rosmarinus S,E
Rosemary
Aromatic shrubs for mixing with others or growing as a decorative hedge set 60cm apart. The leaves are linear, green on top and white beneath. The tubular, white, mauve or pale blue flowers are borne in small clusters from late spring until autumn. They like any well-drained soil and a sunny position. Most usually grown are the varieties of *Rosmarinus officinalis* (**86**), with a height and spread of 1·5 to 2m. Propagate by 15- to 20-cm cuttings in the open in autumn. Prune to remove dead growths and shorten straggly growth in late spring.

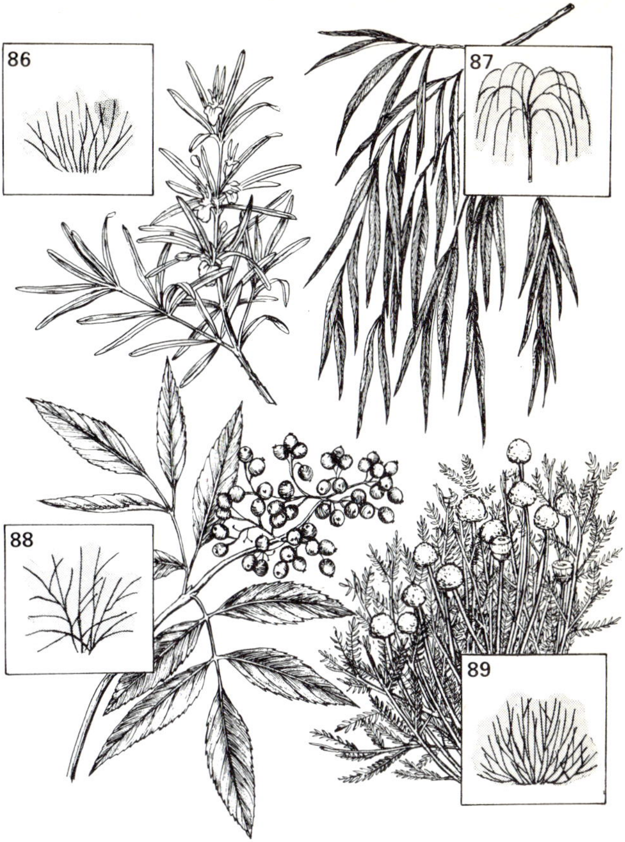

Salix T,S,D
Willow
A handsome genus of trees, with rounded or weeping top growth, and shrubs which are bushy or prostrate growers. They are fast-growing and like moist soil in a sunny position. The lanceolate leaves are green or greyish. In spring, male and female flowers are borne on separate plants, the male ones being showy silky oval catkins and the females inconspicuous and green. In addition the stems and bark are often colourful in winter. Among the various forms are *Salix alba, S.* x *chrysocoma* (**87**), *S. daphnoides, S. matsudana, S. repens* and *S.* 'Wehrhahnii' and some of their varieties. The small forms grow to a height and spread of between 80cm to 2·5m, and the trees up to 20m by 8m. Propagate by 25- to 30-cm cuttings in winter in the open. Prune to remove dead wood, and cut back hard those with coloured stems in late winter.

Sambucus S,D
Elder
Useful for growing in any soil in sun or light shade as specimen shrubs. The compound leaves, composed of lanceolate, sometimes toothed leaflets, are green, yellow or variegated. White or yellow clusters of flowers are borne in summer, followed by black, blue or red fruits in autumn. The three species grown are *Sambucus canadensis, S. nigra* and *S. racemosa* (**88**) and their varieties. Height and spread is between 2 and 3m. Propagation is by 30-cm long early winter cuttings in the open or 10-cm summer heel cuttings in a cold frame. Prune hard in spring to give new growths and better leaf colour.

Santolina S,E
Lavender Cotton
Useful dwarf, aromatic, compact shrubs for the rockery, front of border or low hedges (set 30cm apart), they like any soil except a hot, dry position. The leaves are usually silver-grey, occasionally green, and very finely divided. Clusters of button-like bright yellow flowers are produced in summer. Three species—*Santolina chamaecyparissus*

(**89**), *S. neapolitana* and *S. virens*—and their varieties are usually grown. The height and spread of them all are below 1m. Propagate by 5- to 7·5-cm cuttings in late summer in a cold frame. Prune back hard after flowering or in spring to encourage new basal growths, and clip hedges to shape as required.

Senecio S,E
Although there are annual, perennial and succulent species, two of the shrubby species are popular hardy silver leafed evergreens, useful for mixed shrub borders and low hedges, set 45cm apart. They grow well in any soil, particularly near the sea, and like a sunny or lightly shaded position. The leaves are usually ovate and clusters of yellow daisy-like flowers are borne in summer. *Senecio greyii* and *S. laxifolius* (**90**) are the two species commonly grown, and their height and spread is 1 to 1·5m. Propagate by 7·5- to 10-cm cuttings in late summer in a cold frame. Prune to remove straggly shoots and dead flower heads as necessary, and shape hedges by cutting back old flowering shoots near to the base in autumn.

Skimmia S,E
Hardy, evergreen, slow-growing shrubs which do well in good, well-drained soil and a position of sun or light shade, with some shelter from other plants to protect young foliage from frosts. The leaves are ovate or lanceolate, green, and aromatic. Male and female flowers are usually borne on separate plants in mid- to late spring and these are creamy white or pink,

star-like, fragrant and arranged in spikes. To ensure autumn and winter bright red berries both male and female forms should be planted, unless *Skimmia reevesiana* (syn. *S. fortunei*), the hermaphrodite species, is grown. *S. japonica* (**91**) and its varieties are most usually planted. Height and spread are about 1 to 1·5m. Propagate by 7·5-cm heel cuttings in summer in a cold frame, or seeds sown in autumn in a cold frame. Pruning is usually unnecessary.

Sorbus T,D
Mountain Ash, Rowan Tree, Whitebeam
Easily grown, compact trees as specimens for any garden, producing leaf, flower and fruit colour over a long period. They grow well in any soil, in sun or light shade. The leaves are either ovate (*Sorbus aria*), or more usually compound with lanceolate or ovate leaflets, are green, often with grey undersurfaces, and frequently turn red, yellow, orange or russet in autumn. The white or cream plate-like clusters of small flowers are borne in late spring and early summer and followed by long lasting red, orange, pink, yellow or white berries. *Sorbus aria* and its varieties are Whitebeams, and the Mountain Ashes and Rowans usually grown are varieties and hybrids of *S. aucuparia* (**92**), *S. cashmiriana*, *S. hupehensis*, *S.* 'Joseph Rock', *S. reducta* (miniature for rock or heather gardens), *S. sargentiana* and *S. vilmorinii*. Most grow to a height of 6 to 10m with a spread of 3 to 4m. Propagation is by seeds in autumn in a cold frame, but it is best to buy new plants. Pruning is usually unnecessary.

Spiraea S,D
Easily grown genus of decorative shrubs for border or hedging (set 60cm apart) in any deep good soil in a sunny position. The leaves are green, lanceolate or ovate and sometimes sharply toothed. The star-like flowers are white, pink or crimson and borne in clusters or sprays from spring to late summer, according to forms grown. Most usually grown forms are *Spiraea* x *arguta* (**93**), *S. bullata*, *S. japonica* and its varieties, *S.* x *bumalda* 'Anthony Waterer', *S. menziesii* 'Triumphans' and *S. thunbergii*. Height and spread are about 1·5 to 2·5m. Propagation is by 10-cm summer cuttings in a cold frame, 20- to 30-cm autumn cuttings in the open, or division of the roots. Prune to remove old and straggly growths after flowering, and trim hedges as necessary.

Symphoricarpos (syn. Symphoricarpus) S,D
Snowberry
Very easily grown shrubs in any soil in light shade or sun, either in a border or as a hedge, with the plants set 45cm apart. The green leaves are ovate or nearly round The pink bell-shaped flowers are borne in clusters in mid- to late summer and are followed by large pink, purplish crimson or white berries which persist throughout winter. *Symphoricarpos albus* (**94**, syn. *S. racemosus*) and its varieties, *S. orbiculatus*, and *S.* x *chenaultii* and its varieties, are usually grown. Height is about 1·5m and spread the same or rather more. Propagate by removing rooted suckers in winter or 20-cm cuttings in winter in the open. Prune to thin out unwanted growth and remove suckers in winter, and trim hedges as necessary in summer.

Syringa T,S,D
Lilac
Useful late spring flowering small trees (standards with a bare stem of about 1m) or shrubs for borders, screening, or hedges with plants set 2 to 3m apart. The mid-green leaves are ovate to almost round. The funnel-shaped single or double flowers in many colour shades are borne in loose upright spikes and are usually fragrant. They grow well in good soil in a sunny position, but to get them established remove flower buds the first year. Most commonly grown are the many varieties of *Syringa vulgaris* (**95**), the species *S. chinensis* and *S. persica*, and *S.* x *prestoniae* (Canadian hybrids), all of which grow to a height of 1·5 to 3m and spread of 1 to 1·5m. Two smaller species, growing about 1·5m by 80cm, are *S. microphylla* and *S. velutina* (syn. *S. palibiniana*). Propagation is possible by 7·5- to 10-cm heel cuttings in summer in heat, or the plants can be budded or grafted. It is generally advisable to buy new plants. Prune to remove dead flower heads and unwanted branches.

Tamarix S,D
Tamarisk
A useful genus of shrubs for windbreaks or hedges (set 60cm apart) in coastal areas. They grow well in any chalk-free soil and prefer a sunny position. The leaves are awl-shaped, green or greyish and carried like plumes. The flowers are shades of pink, sometimes fragrant and borne in graceful sprays from early summer to autumn, according to species or variety. The three species grown are *Tamarix gallica*, *T. pentandra* (**96**, syn. *T. hispida aestivalis*) and its varieties, and *T. tetrandra*. These have a height and spread of about 3m by 2m. Propagation is

by 30-cm cuttings in autumn in the open. Prune fairly hard *T. gallica* and *T. pentandra* during winter, and *T. tetrandra* after flowering, to keep plants bushy.

Taxus C,T/S,E
Yew
Single or multi-stemmed trees or shrubs. All varieties of *Taxus baccata* (**97**), are usually very long-lived and grow well in any soil and any position. The leaves are needle-like in shades of dark green, yellow or grey. Male and female flowers are borne on separate plants and are inconspicuous; some female forms carry fleshy, red, poisonous fruits in autumn. Height and spread can vary from about 5m down to miniatures growing 45cm high by a spread of 1·5m. This makes taxus a suitable plant for many purposes, such as a specimen tree, hedges (set 45cm apart), an evergreen foil for other shrubs, or plants for rockeries and containers. Propagation is by seeds or 7·5- to 10-cm cuttings, both in autumn in a cold frame. Prune as necessary to maintain shape.

Thuja C,T,E
Arbor-Vitae
Easily grown conifers in most soils, preferably in a sheltered position in full sun. The trees are usually rounded or conical in shape and the leaves, in various shades of green, yellow, and sometimes purple, are like flat scales surrounding the shoots. The cones produced are small, urn-shaped, and yellowish brown. The three species grown—*Thuja occidentalis, T. orientalis* and *T. plicata* (**98**)—reach a height of 15 to 40m and spread of 6m, but there are very many smaller forms suitable as garden specimens, for hedging (set 60cm apart), in rock or heather gardens or for containers. These vary in height and spread from 2m down to 30cm. Propagation is difficult and it is best to buy new plants. No pruning is required except to shape hedges as necessary and to remove tips of shoots to encourage bushiness.

Viburnum S,E,D
A useful genus of shrubs for all gardens, the plants grow well in any moist soil, preferably in full sun. By choosing species and varieties colour and interest can be maintained throughout the year. The green leaves are usually ovate, sometimes lanceolate, evergreen or deciduous and some provide autumn colour. The flowers are usually tubular, pink or white, sometimes fragrant, and are borne in pendant or plate-like clusters from early winter to late spring, according to the form selected. Some types produce autumn berries of blue, red, black or yellow. Among good winter flowering forms are *Viburnum* x *bodnantense* (D), *V. fragrans* (syn. *V. farreri*) (D), and *V. tinus* (Laurustinus, E) and their hybrids and varieties. Spring flowering types include *V. burkwoodii* (E), *V.* x *carlcephalum* (D), *V. carlesii* (D), *V. opulus* 'Sterile' (the Snowball Tree) and *V. tomentosum* (D) and some of their varieties and hybrids. For autumn berries, or coloured foliage or both *V. davidii* (E), *V. henryi* (E), *V. lantana* (D), and *V. opulus* (**99**, Guelder Rose, D) and its varieties are useful. Most grow to a height of 1 to 3m and spread 1 to 2m. Propagate by 7·5- to 10-cm heel cuttings in early autumn in a cold frame, or by layering in early autumn. Prune as necessary, evergreens in late spring and deciduous forms after flowering.

Vinca S,E
Greater and Lesser Periwinkles
Very useful trailing evergreens for ground cover, banks, shady positions and 'wild' garden areas. They grow well in any well-drained soil in shade or light shade. The leaves are ovate or lanceolate, green or variegated green, yellow and white. The flowers are tubular to flat in shades of blue, purple, mauve or white and appear at intervals from late spring to early autumn. The two species commonly grown are *Vinca major* (**100**), height 15 to 30cm and spread indefinite, and *V. minor*, height 5 to 10cm and spread also indefinite; there are a number of varieties of both. Propagation is by division during winter. Pruning is unnecessary except to restrict spread if required.

Vitis Cl,D
Grape Vine, Ornamental Vine
Mainly grown for the brilliant autumn colours of their large coarsely toothed, ovate or three- to five-lobed compound leaves, the foliage is dark green when young. Black, purple or red 'grapes' are produced after insignificant white, fragrant, early summer flower clusters. They are particularly useful for covering walls, arches, unsightly trees or growing up trellis to which they attach themselves by tendrils. They like a rich, deep soil, preferably with lime added, and sun or light shade. The species usually grown, *Vitis coignetiae* and *V. vinifera* (**101**) and its varieties, grow about 5 to 6m high and spread as far as allowed. Propagate by autumn layering the first species and taking 10- to 15-cm cuttings in summer in heat of the second. Prune to encourage spreading by cutting back young plants to 30cm after planting, after which thin out shoots as necessary and

cut back side growths in late summer.

Weigela (syn. Diervilla) S,D
Useful and reliable summer flowering shrubs for a good well-drained soil, in a sunny or lightly shaded position, for growing in borders, against walls and fences, on banks and for low screening. The leaves are ovate and usually green but sometimes purple or variegated green and yellow. The tubular pink or red flowers are borne in clusters in early summer. Most usually grown are *Weigela florida* (**102**) and its varieties, and a number of hybrids such as 'Bristol Ruby' and 'Newport Red'. Height and spread are 1·5 to 2m. Propagate by 7·5- to 10-cm heel cuttings in early summer in a cold frame or 30-cm cuttings in autumn in the open. Prune a few old stems hard back each year after flowering.

Wisteria (syn. Wistaria) Cl,D
Very popular climbers for walls, fences, trees, arches, pergolas, they need an ordinary soil but prefer a sunny position. The pale or mid-green leaves are compound and composed of many leaflets, sometimes with a silvery sheen. The mauve, violet, pink or white flowers, sometimes fragrant, are borne in long, drooping sprays in late spring and early summer, usually before the leaves appear. Most often grown are *Wisteria floribunda*, *W. sinensis* (**103**) and *W. venusta* and their varieties. Mature height can be 4 to 30m and spread according to training. Propagation by layering or by 7·5- to 10-cm heel cuttings in summer in heat. Prune back side shoots in summer to about 15cm and remove unwanted growths.

Glossary

Acid soil: soil with a pH of less than 7 which is deficient in lime.
Adult foliage: leaves borne by a mature plant which differ in shape and other characteristics from early leaves.
Alkaline soil: soil with a pH of more than 7 which is deficient in acidic humus and some essential chemicals.
Alpine: plant that grows in the wild between the tree and snow lines of mountains. Often called rock plant.
Annual: plant which completes its life-cycle in one season from seed to seed and then dies.
Bacteria: minute simple forms of life found in the soil. Most are beneficial to plants and soil if the ground is well cultivated.
Bare-rooted: new plants without soil round their roots.
Bicolour: flower with petals of more than one colour.
Bract: a modified leaf at the base of a flower stem, on the stem of a cluster of flowers, or part of the flower head, often brightly coloured.
Bud: an embryo shoot or flower.
Calyx: outer whorl of sepals that protect the flower bud as it opens.
Chlorophyll: green pigment used by plants in photosynthesis.
Compost: two meanings. One, a special mixture of peat, sand, loam or other ingredients for growing seeds, cuttings and plants in containers. Two: rotted down vegetable or animal waste (often referred to as manure) to give humus-forming material.
Conifer: tree bearing cones, and any member of the *Coniferae* class.
Container grown: plants in containers of compost for planting any time of year.
Corolla: whorl of petals, usually coloured, inside the calyx.
Cross-pollination: the transference of pollen from the flower of one plant to another plant. Often used to produce new varieties.
Cutting: piece, usually of stem, cut from a living plant and used to form a new plant identical to its parent.
Deadheading: removing dead flowers from plants.
Deciduous: plant which loses its leaves at the end of the growing season.
Dormant: period when plant makes little or no new growth, usually in winter.
Double: flower with more than a single whorl of petals.
Double digging: digging both the top and lower spits of soil.
Evergreen: plant which has leaves all year round.
Eye: two meanings. One, the centre of a flower when it is of a different colour to the petals. Two, a growth bud.
Foliage: leaves of a plant.
Foliar feeding: applying diluted liquid fertilizer to plant leaves.
Formal garden: garden designed on geometrical lines.
Fungicide: chemical used for preventing or killing fungus diseases of plants.
Fungus: very simple organisms which live on plants and cause them to become diseased or assist in the decay of plants already dead. Spread mainly by microscopic spores ('flowers').
Genera: plural of genus.
Genus: group of similar plants including one or more species.
Germination: first stages of seed growth to form a new plant.
Glaucous: term used to describe the bluish-green or bloom-covered appearance of stems and leaves.
Ground cover: low-growing or prostrate plants set between others to look ornamental and to smother weeds.
Harden-off: gradually giving plants raised in warm conditions colder growing environments until they are acclimatized sufficiently to be planted outdoors.
Heel-in: put plants in a trench in a protected site until ready for planting.
Herbaceous plant: plant with non-woody stems.
Herbicide: chemical for killing weeds, usually called weedkillers.
Hermaphrodite: flowers which have both male and female organs.
Hip (or hep): the fruit of a rose.
Humus: well-rotted residue of animal and vegetable waste matter which is essential for good soil structure.
Hybrid: result of crossing two varieties or species to give a plant which may be superior to either of its parents.
Informal garden: natural type garden with irregular lines.
Insecticide: chemical to kill insect pests. Insecticides work by killing on contact or by being absorbed systemically into the plant's sap stream so the insects are killed when they suck the sap.
Juvenile foliage: leaves of a young tree which are quite different from the adult foliage.
Leaflet: one of the small leaves of a compound leaf.
Leafmould: the rotted down residue of dead leaves.
Mixed border: area where different types of plants are grown together.
Mulch: layer of organic matter spread on soil to conserve moisture and smother weeds.

Native: plant that grows wild naturally in the country of origin.
Nectar: sweet substance secreted by some flowers to attract insects to aid pollination.
Neutral: soil that is neither acid nor alkaline.
Node: stem joint, usually swollen, from which leaves, shoots and buds arise.
Ovary: the part of the flower enclosing the ovules which, when fertilized, form seeds.
Panicle: flower cluster with many-stalked flowers on small separate branches.
Parasite: living organism which lives on another organism, e.g. fungus on a plant.
Perianth: the ring of sepals and petals, or one or other, which surround the reproductive parts of the flower.
Petal: single coloured modified 'leaf' which forms part of the protection for the inner parts of the flower.
Pesticides: chemicals for killing either insect pests or diseases.
pH: scale used to express the acidity or alkalinity of soil.
Photosynthesis: the method by which plants use the energy from sunlight to convert simple chemicals into carbohydrates and proteins, giving off oxygen as a waste product.
Pollen: dust-like particles carrying the male sex cells for pollination.
Pollination: transference of pollen to the female parts (pistil) of the same or another flower.
Potting-on: removing plants and compost from a small pot to a larger one with more compost to allow further growth.
Propagation: increasing plants by cuttings, layering, grafting, seeds or division from a parent plant.
Prostrate: plant that grows close to the ground.
Pruning: cutting back the shoots of plants to maintain their shapes and to get rid of damaged, diseased or dead growth and encourage fresh growth.
Receptacle: thickened end of flower stalk from which the various parts of the flower arise.
Seedling: young plant after seed germination with a single stem and usually one pair of leaves.
Semi-evergreen: plant that will keep all or some of its leaves under favourable weather and growing conditions.
Sepal: modified leaf, usually green, which forms part of the calyx.
Serrated: toothed margins of leaves.
Single: flower with the normal number of petals.
Species: one or more very similar plants within a genus.
Specimen plant: plant grown on its own to be viewed from all sides.
Spit: soil dug to the depth of the spade blade or fork tines.
Stamen: male reproductive organ of a plant producing pollen.
Standard: tree or shrub trained to grow on a bare stem a metre or more high.
Stigma: part of flower's female organs on which pollen is deposited.
Sub-soil: soil below the top 30cm.
Sucker: shoot growth direct from the roots of the plant.
Synonym: alternative plant name.
'Take': when cuttings root, or new plants start producing fresh roots and shoots.
Tendril: modified stem or leaf which twists round support to enable plant to climb upwards.
Terminal: top shoot, flower or leaf.
Tilth: crumbly surface layer of soil after raking or hoeing.
Top soil: top 30cm of soil.
Topiary: shrubs, usually evergreen, which are clipped and trained into decorative shapes.
Transplanting: moving young plants to give them more space for growth or establish them in another place.
Truss: cluster of flowers or fruits.
Underplant: putting low-growing plants round and between tall-growing plants, like ground cover.
Unisexual: flower of a particular plant which is of one sex only.
Variegated: leaves (sometimes petals) that are marked, spotted or patterned in one or more different colours.
Variety: distinct form of a species.
Woodland garden: mixture of trees, shrubs and other plants grown as naturally as possible within garden limitations.

Book list

There are many books about trees, shrubs and climbers, and gardening in general. A good bookshop should stock most of the current titles, and those listed below are but a few available.

Hilliers' Manual of Trees and Shrubs, Hillier Nurseries (Winchester) Ltd, Ampfield House, Ampfield, Romsey, Hants, SO5 9PA. Hardback £6.50 (+ 80p post and packing), or softcover £3.00 (+ 80p post and packing).
A detailed guide to trees, shrubs and climbers with good descriptions of the more common as well as the unusual genera grown in this country. It also contains lists of plants suitable for particular situations.

Shrubs for Your Garden, Peter Seabrook, Floraprint Ltd, £4.95
A very useful book which contains information and illustrations in colour of the commonly, and not so commonly, grown shrubs in English gardens. The first section is devoted to the uses and care of shrubs.

Trees for Your Garden, Roy Lancaster, Floraprint Ltd, £4.95
A companion book to the one previously listed which has a similarly colourful layout and informative text about trees in the garden. Cultural instructions are also included.

Reader's Digest Encyclopaedia of Garden Plants and Flowers, Reader's Digest, London, £8.95
Although expensive, it contains detailed information about garden plants, including trees, shrubs and climbers. The A-Z layout makes for easy reference and it is comprehensively illustrated in colour and black and white.

Roses—A Selected List of Varieties, Royal National Rose Society, Bone Hill, Chiswell Green Lane, St. Albans, Hertfordshire. 40p (plus 10p post and packing)
An A-Z of varieties selected by the Royal National Rose Society with descriptions of each and the various types of roses. It also has a useful section of lists of roses for special purposes.

The Collingridge Encyclopedia of Gardening, Arthur Hellyer, Hamlyn, London, £8.95
Broadly divided into two A-Z sections, one covering garden plants, the other garden management, this extremely informative book also incorporates sections on associating plants, garden design and fruit and vegetables. Illustrations are in black and white, and the layout and text are easy to follow.

MAGAZINES
There are several gardening magazines and a subscription to one or more of them can prove helpful in supplying up-to-date information about trees, shrubs and climbers and how to grow them.

Amateur Gardening, IPC Magazines Ltd, Kings Reach Tower, Stamford Street, London SE1 9LS. 15p. Weekly.

Flora, Stanley Gibbons Magazines Ltd, Drury House, Russell Street, London WC2B 5HD. 50p. Quarterly.

Garden News, EMAP National Publications Ltd, 117 Park Road, Peterborough PE1 2TS. 15p. Weekly.

The Garden, Journal of the Royal Horticultural Society, Vincent Square, London SW1P 2PE. 65p (or free to members). Monthly.

Popular Gardening, IPC Magazines Ltd, Kings Reach Tower, Stamford Street, London SE1 9LS. 15p. Weekly.

Practical Gardening, EMAP National Publications Ltd, Aqua House, London Road, Peterborough PE2 8AQ. 35p. Monthly.

Societies

Many gardeners feel it helpful to belong to one or more gardening societies. Local ones have the advantage of being close to home and useful for getting helpful information about plants, and often an exchange of them. Other benefits include cheaper plants, seeds and fertilizers as they can be bought in bulk by the society.

The most important of all national societies is the Royal Horticultural Society, Vincent Square, London SW1P 2PE. As a member you are entitled to visit the Chelsea Flower Show on the private viewing day, go to any or all of the 15 other flower shows held at Vincent Square during the year, visit the Society's Wisley Garden in Surrey (including lectures and demonstrations), receive **The Garden** magazine free each month, receive advice on identification of plants, pests and diseases free from the Wisley laboratory, subject to certain fees have your soil analysed or garden inspected, attend lectures held in conjunction with the shows, use the Society's library, participate in the annual seed distribution from Wisley Garden, and vote at all Society meetings.

Other societies connected with growing trees, shrubs and climbers and which often hold shows and exhibitions in conjunction with the Royal Horticultural Society include:

British Fuchsia Society
Heather Society
International Camellia Society
Ivy Society
Royal National Rose Society

Details of these societies may be obtained from their secretaries and, if you are unable to obtain their names and addresses locally, the Royal Horticultural Society will generally be able to assist. Send a s.a.e. for a reply.

Suppliers

Due to the high cost of packing and carriage of trees, shrubs and climbers direct from nurserymen, more and more have become garden centres where you can browse at leisure and make your personal choice, thus cutting out additional costs.

Listed below are some of the well-known firms who still produce catalogues and are willing to fulfill your orders for delivery to your home. The ones selected have comprehensive lists and should be able to supply most of the plants listed in the A-Z section. Due to the cost of production of the catalogues, a charge may be made for them.

Bressingham Gardens,
Diss,
Norfolk IP22 2AB

County Park Nursery,
Essex Gardens,
Hornchurch,
Essex

Hilliers Nurseries (Winchester) Ltd,
Ampfield House,
Ampfield,
Romsey,
Hants S05 9PA

Knap Hill Nursery Ltd,
Barrs Lane,
Knaphill,
Woking,
Surrey GU21 2JW

E. B. Le Grice (Roses) Ltd,
Norwich Road,
North Walsingham,
Norfolk NR28 0DR

Notcutts Nurseries Ltd,
Woodbridge,
Suffolk IP12 4AF

Pennell & Sons Ltd,
Princess Street,
Lincoln LN5 7QL

G. Reuthe Ltd,
The Nurseries,
Jackass Lane,
Keston,
Kent BR2 6AW

Robinsons Gardens Ltd,
Rushmoor Hill Nurseries,
Knockholt,
Sevenoaks,
Kent TN14 7NN

L. R. Russell Ltd,
Richmond Nurseries,
Windlesham,
Surrey GU20 6LL

Scotts Nurseries (Merriott) Ltd,
Merriott,
Somerset

South Downs Nurseries,
Southgate Street,
Redruth,
Cornwall

Toynbees Nurseries,
Barnham,
Nr Bognor Regis,
West Sussex

Conversion tables

Length

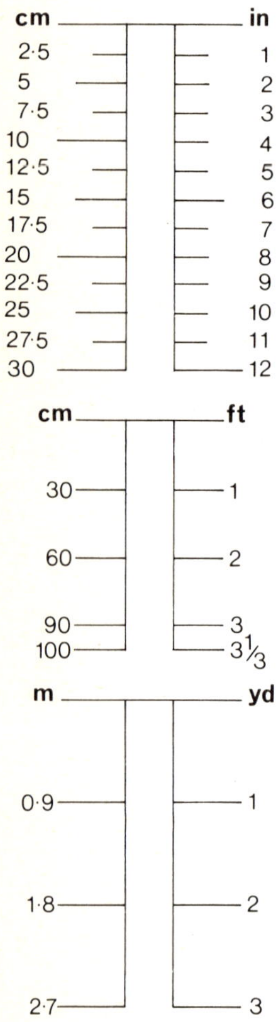

Area

1sq cm = 0.15sq in
6.45sq cm = 1sq in
1sq m = 10.76sq ft/ 1.19sq yd
4046sq m = 1 acre
1 hectare = 2.47 acres

Weight

1g = 0.035oz
28.35g = 1oz
100g = 3.5oz
454g = 1lb
500g = 17.5oz
1kg = 2.21lb
6.35kg = 1 stone/14lb
50.80kg = 1cwt/112lb
1.02 tonnes = 1 ton

Capacity and Volume

500ml = 0.88pt
568ml = 1pt
1000ml = 1.76pt
1 litre = 35.19fl oz
4.55 litres = 1gal
10 litres (1dl) = 2.2gal
1 bushel/8gal = 36.37 litres
100 litres = 22gal
1cu cm = 0.06cu in
1cu dm = 0.035cu ft
1cu m = 1.31cu yd

Abbreviations

sq = square
g = gram
oz = ounce
kg = kilogram
lb = pound
cwt = hundredweight
ml = millilitre (=cc)
pt = pint
l = litre
fl oz = fluid ounce
dl = decolitre
gal = gallon
hl = hectolitre
cu = cubic
dm = decimetre
cm = centimetre
mm = millimetre
m = metre
in = inch
ft = foot
yd = yard

Temperature

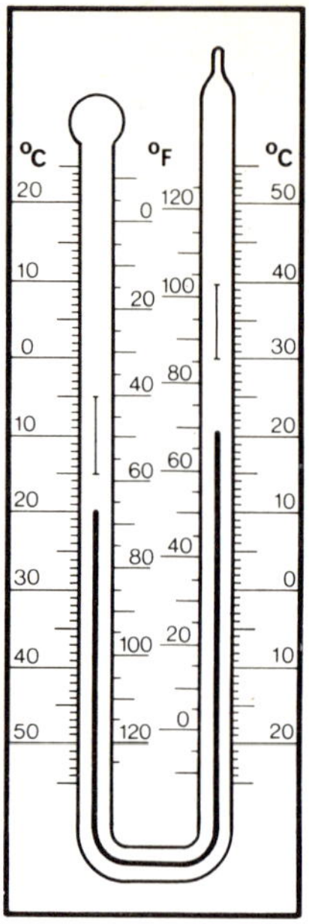

▲ A maximum and minimum thermometer is used to record the highest and lowest temperatures every 24 hours.

°F = °Fahrenheit
°C = °Celcius (Centigrade)
* = freezing point

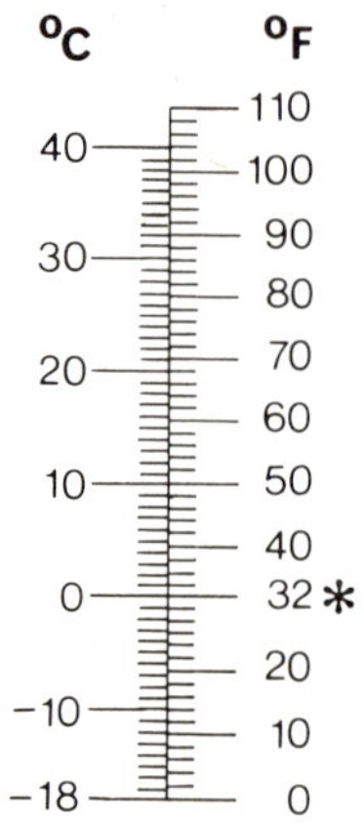

Index of common names

Numbers in italics refer to illustrations.

Index

Numbers in italics refer to illustrations.

Credits

Artists
Pamela Dowson
Ron Hayward Art Group
Kate Lloyd-Jones

Photographs
A-Z Collection: 13(bl)
Mary Evans: 7
Christina Gascoigne/Robert Harding Associates: 6
Neil Holmes: 19, 25, 33, 53
Tania Midgeley: 13(top)
Roger Perry: 42
Popperphoto: 48
Harry Smith: 2, 15(br, tr), 21, 22, 23, 48(bl, tr), 49

Cover
Design: Barry Kemp
Photograph: Jeremy Whitaker

The publishers would also like to thank the following for their help in producing this book: Ken and Vera Goodbun, Malcolm Smythe and Rassells Garden Centre, London.